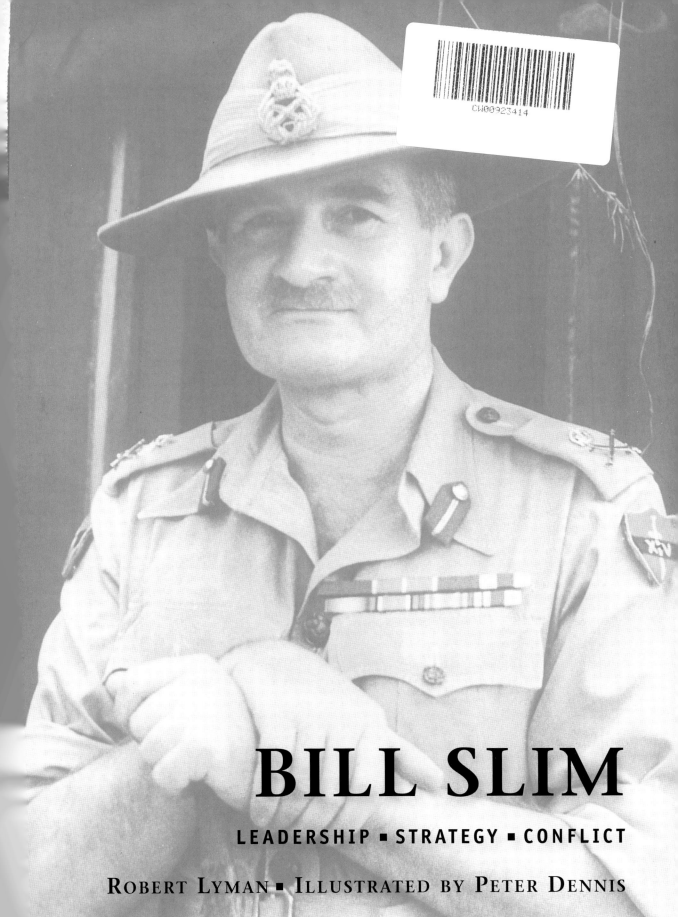

# BILL SLIM

## LEADERSHIP ▪ STRATEGY ▪ CONFLICT

ROBERT LYMAN ▪ ILLUSTRATED BY PETER DENNIS

First published in Great Britain in 2011 by Osprey Publishing,
Midland House, West Way, Botley, Oxford OX2 0PH, UK
44-02 23rd St, Suite 219, Long Island City, NY 11101, USA

E-mail: info@ospreypublishing.com

OSPREY PUBLISHING IS PART OF THE OSPREY GROUP

A CIP catalogue record for this book is available from the British Library.

ISBN: 978 1 84908 528 1
E-book ISBN: 978 1 84908 529 8

Editorial by Ilios Publishing Ltd, Oxford, UK (www.iliospublishing.com)
Page layout by Myriam Bell Design, France
Index by Marie-Pierre Evans
Typeset in Stone Serif and Officina Sans
Maps by Mapping Specialists Ltd
Originated by PDQ Digital Media Solutions Ltd, Suffolk
Printed in Hong Kong through Worldprint Ltd.

11 12 13 14 15   10 9 8 7 6 5 4 3 2 1

## Acknowledgements

To Ian C. Pearson, who provided the photographs of Slim in
Mesopotamia, taken by his great uncle, Captain A. C. Pearson.

### Imperial War Museum Collections

The photographs in this book come from the Imperial War Museum's
huge collections, which cover all aspects of conflict involving Britain
and the Commonwealth since the start of the 20th century. These
rich resources are available online to search, browse and buy at
www.iwmcollections.org.uk. In addition to collections online, you
can visit the visitor rooms where you can explore over 8 million
photographs, thousands of hours of moving images, the largest sound
archive of its kind in the world, thousands of diaries and letters written
by people in wartime and a huge reference library. To make an
appointment, call (020) 7416 5320, or e-mail mail@iwm.org.uk.

www.iwm.org.uk

### Artist's note

Readers may care to note that the original paintings from which the
colour plates in this book were prepared are available for private sale.
The Publishers retain all reproduction copyright whatsoever. All
enquiries should be addressed to:

Peter Dennis, Fieldhead, the Park, Mansfield, NOTTS, NG18 2AT, UK

The Publishers regret that they can enter into no correspondence upon
this matter.

### Front cover image

© Trinity Mirror / Mirrorpix / Alamy

### The Woodland Trust

Osprey Publishing are supporting the Woodland Trust, the UK's leading
woodland conservation charity, by funding the dedication of trees.

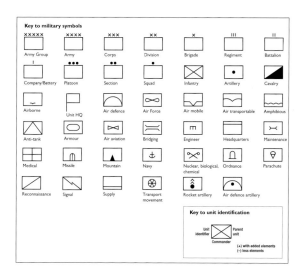

# CONTENTS

# INTRODUCTION

Every cadet at Britain's Royal Military Academy at Sandhurst receives, on joining, a thin red volume entitled *Serve To Lead*. Bearing the motto of the Academy, the book distils the wisdom of past British military leaders (not all of whom are famous) on the subject of morale and leadership in war. For most cadets this is their first exposure to Field Marshal Sir 'Bill' Slim (he was never called William), the man responsible for destroying two Japanese armies during World War II, the first in India, around Imphal and Kohima, in 1944 and the second in Burma, around Meiktila and Mandalay, in 1945.

Every analysis of Slim's achievements in Burma provides evidence of a remarkable military talent. Most are effusive in their praise for him as a military commander.

In a masterful summary of the higher command of the Burma Campaign, the historian Frank McLynn states:

There are solid grounds for asserting that when due allowances have been made… Slim's encirclement of the Japanese on the Irrawaddy deserves to rank with the great military achievements of all time – Alexander at Gaugamela in 331 BC, Hannibal at Cannae (216 BC), Julius Caesar at Alesia (58 BC), the Mongol general Subudei at Mohi (1241) or Napoleon at Austerlitz (1805). The often made – but actually ludicrous – comparison between Montgomery and Slim is relevant here… there is no Montgomery equivalent of the Irrawaddy campaign. His one attempt to prove himself a master of the war of movement – Operation MARKET GARDEN against Arnhem – was a signal and embarrassing failure. Montgomery was a military talent; Slim was a military genius.[1]

And yet, in 1942 Bill Slim was a relatively unknown and not particularly successful

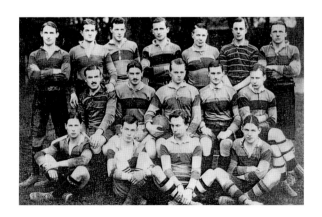

1. Frank McLynn *The Burma Campaign* (London: Bodley Head, 2010), p. 432.

Indian Army general who had just presided over the British Army's longest ever retreat, 1,000 miles (1,600km) from Burma into India. How did he find himself in command of a triumphant, all-conquering army in India in 1944 and Burma in 1945? The story of the transformation of this army, from defeat into victory, the title of his best-selling war memoir in 1956, is not just the story of British arms in the Far East between 1942 and 1945, but the account of Slim's rise to military greatness. At the end of the war he commanded the largest British military force ever assembled, and at Imphal in 1944 (to say nothing of Mandalay–Meiktila in 1945) had dealt what one Japanese commentator, a veteran diplomat, considered to be the greatest defeat Japan had ever suffered in its history.[2]

Slim was successful as a commander for two reasons. He was, first and foremost, a born leader of men. He was constantly mindful of the predicament of the men who had to fight battles designed by men who would often be far to the rear when the bullets began to fly. Slim instinctively knew that the strength of an army lies not in its equipment or its officers, but in the training and morale of its soldiers. His basic premise was:

> That the fighting capacity of every unit is based upon the faith of soldiers in their leaders; that discipline begins with the officer and spreads downward from him to the soldier; that genuine comradeship in arms is achieved when all ranks do more than is required of them…. In battle, the soldier has only his sense of duty, and his sense of shame. These are the things which make men go on fighting even though terror grips their heart. Every soldier, therefore, must be instilled with pride in his unit and in himself, and to do this he must be treated with justice and respect.

Slim made tremendous efforts to communicate with his men, travelling vast distances to talk with them, simply and honestly, as man to man. He never engaged in histrionics or tricks of oratory and through these events his strong and attractive personality shone through. His firm view was that the most important attribute of a leader was his effect on morale, and he did everything he could to ensure that he was seen and trusted by his men. He inspired confidence because he related to the men as men, not as subordinates. He was the antithesis of the 'château general' who never ventured far from the comfort of his headquarters, far to the rear of the action. He brought his men into his confidence in a way that was very unusual at the time, the result of the complete absence in his personal make-up of any social pretension. Half a century after the war George Macdonald Fraser, the best-selling author of the 'Flashman' books, recalled Slim arriving at his battalion of the Border Regiment in Burma in 1945 for one of these talks:

> The biggest boost to morale was the burly man who came to talk to the assembled battalion by the lake shore – I'm not sure when, but it was

---

2. Toshikazu Kase *Eclipse of the Rising Sun* (London: Jonathan Cape, 1951), p. 92.

unforgettable. Slim was like that: the only man I've ever seen who had a force that came out of him, a strength of personality that I've puzzled over since.... His appearance was plain enough: large, heavily built, grim-faced with that hard mouth and bulldog chin; the rakish Gurkha hat was at odds with the slung carbine and untidy trouser bottoms.... Nor was he an orator.... His delivery was blunt, matter-of-fact, without gestures or mannerisms, only a lack of them. He knew how to make an entrance – or rather, he probably didn't, and it came naturally… Slim emerged from under the trees by the lake shore, there was no nonsense of 'gather round' or jumping on boxes; he just stood with his thumb hooked in his carbine sling and talked about how we had caught Jap off-balance and were going to annihilate him in the open; there was no exhortation or ringing clichés, no jokes or self-conscious use of barrack-room slang – when he called the Japs 'bastards' it was casual and without heat. He was telling us informally what would be, in the reflective way of intimate conversation. And we believed every word – and it all came true. I think it was that sense of being close to us, as though he were chatting offhand to an understanding nephew (not for nothing was he 'Uncle Bill') that was his great gift.... You knew, when he talked of smashing the Jap, that to him it meant not only arrows on a map but clearing bunkers and going in under shell-fire; that he had the head of a general with the heart of a private soldier.[3]

Slim knew his men and could communicate with them because he was one of them, and, from the bloody days in Gallipoli and Mesopotamia during World War I and in the inter-war years on the North-West Frontier, had experienced their bitterest trials. 'He understood men' wrote the Australian journalist Ronald McKie, who met him in Burma. 'He spoke their language as he moved among them, from forward positions to training bases. He had the richest of common-sense, a dour soldier's humour and a simple earthy wisdom. Wherever he moved he lifted morale. He was the finest of Englishmen.'[4] Frank Owen, the Fleet Street editor who watched him closely in India and Burma for two years, observed: 'Slim does not court popularity, and he hates publicity. But he inspires trust. The man cares deeply for his troops, and they are well aware that their well-being is his permanent priority.'[5]

In addition to giving them the mental and practical wherewithal to fight the Japanese, one of the most fearsome armies the British have ever had to face, Slim

At Mandalay, April 1945. Savouring the moment of his victory, the battles of Meiktila and Mandalay in March 1945, Slim has every reason to be pleased at the utter destruction of Kimura's army in what the latter called the 'masterstroke' of British strategy. Slung over his shoulder was an M1 carbine, given to him as a gift by General Joe Stilwell. (Alamy, B4WF7J)

3. George MacDonald Fraser *Quartered Safe Out Here* (London: Harper Collins, 1992), p. 37.

4. Ronald McKie *Echoes from Forgotten Wars* (Sydney: Collins, 1980) p. 117.

5. Frank Owen 'Slim' in *Phoenix Magazine* (New Delhi: South East Asia Command, 1945).

took many practical steps to improve his men's health and welfare. His approach to the building up of the fighting power of an army – from a situation of profound defeat and in the face of crippling resource constraints – was built on the twin platforms of rigorous training and development of each individual's will to win, through a deeply thought-out programme of support designed to meet the physical, intellectual and spiritual needs of each fighting man.

As a result the men of Fourteenth Army – British, Indian, African and Gurkha – gave him their loyalty in a way rarely seen in the annals of command. It would be inconceivable to think of Field Marshal Montgomery as 'Uncle Bernard', but it was in 'Uncle Bill' that soldiers in Burma, from the dark days of 1942 and 1943 through to the great victories over the Japanese in 1944 and 1945, put their confidence. Brigadier Bernard Fergusson observed that he 'was the only Indian Army general of my acquaintance that ever got himself across to British troops. Monosyllables do not usually carry a cadence; but to thousands of British troops, as well as to Indians and to his own beloved Gurkhas, there will always be a special magic in the words "Bill Slim".'[6]

Slim's second legacy was his approach to warfare, which at the time was very different to received wisdom across the British armed forces. He was not a theoretician of war, although after the war he became for a short time Commandant of the Royal College of Defence Studies. Rather, he was an intensely practical strategist. At his heart he was a proponent of the maxim taught to him when he was a young officer by a hoary old sergeant-major: 'Hit the other fellow as quick as you can and as hard as you can, where it hurts him most, when he ain't looking.'[7] Slim's entire approach to strategy was to exploit his enemy's weaknesses and so undermine his will to win. He did this successfully in Syria, India and Burma by concentrating force to achieve surprise, psychological shock and physical momentum. By so doing he attempted to achieve moral dominance on the battlefield over his enemy. It was an approach to war that sat in stark contrast to the idea of matching strength with strength, and force with force, where the goal of strategy was simply to slog it out with an enemy in an attritional confrontation of the sort expounded by less imaginative commanders (British and others) elsewhere during the war and, indeed, throughout history. Slim prized above all the virtues of cunning and guile, and he sought opportunities at every turn to trick and deceive his enemy. In the fighting in India and Burma this required realistic,

Outside 10 Downing Street after a Cabinet meeting, 1950. Slim was a successful CIGS during the turbulent post-war period that included National Service, the establishment of NATO and the Korean War. (Corbis, U1156405INP)

---

6. Lord Ballantrae 'Slim' *The Army Quarterly*, (Volume 4, 1971), p. 268

7. William Slim *Defeat into Victory* (London: Cassells, 1956), p. 551. All other unattributed quotations from Slim are taken from this work.

physically demanding training; the use of air power to supply forward troops; new tactics to fight the Japanese; the delegation of command to the lowest possible level; a self-help approach to logistical deficiencies and a relentless exploitation of the pursuit, to ensure that an enemy caught off guard had limited opportunities to recover its equilibrium. The campaigns in India and Burma in 1944 and 1945 were to reward Slim's approach to warfare with a victory that few if any in 1942 or 1943 foresaw.

Above: 'Slim's Lambs', with Slim in the middle of the back row. While he was at King Edward's his status as an uncertificated elementary teacher allowed him entry to the Birmingham University Officers' Training Corps (OTC), which he joined in 1912. He soon reached the exalted rank of lance-corporal. (Viscount Slim)

# THE EARLY YEARS

Slim had always wanted to be a soldier, but his birth in 1891 into a lower middle-class family in Bishopton, Bristol, would have stifled these ambitions were it not for the onset of World War I. By this time his family was living in Birmingham, and after leaving King Edward's School the young Slim had found himself teaching at a primary school before, in 1910, beginning work as a clerk in Stewarts & Lloyds, a metal-tube maker. Military aspirations never far from the fore, Slim wangled his way into the Birmingham University Officers' Training Corps in 1912 (even though he was not at the University), and was thus able to be commissioned as a temporary second lieutenant in the Royal Warwickshire Regiment on 22 August 1914.

It was with the Warwicks that, on 8 August 1915, he was badly wounded by a Turkish machine gun while attempting, at the head of his very depleted company, to storm Hill 971 on the Sari Bair Ridge, the long spine that ran along the peninsula and dominated the surrounding countryside running down to the sparkling Aegean. The slopes of the extensive Sari Bair position were of steep, bare, sandy rock, interspersed with patches of scrub thorn. Below the spine a mass of confusing nullahs and ravines undulated wildly,

Below: With Birmingham University OTC. (Viscount Slim)

confusing even the most competent subaltern possessed of a map and compass. By the time the Warwicks reached the start point of the brigade attack, the men of 1st Battalion, 6th Gurkha Rifles, to their right, Slim's company had been reduced to 50 men and he was its third commander in 48 hours. They were all dog tired. 'For three nights and two days' he later wrote, 'with very little sleep, not much food and less water, we had scrambled, climbed and wandered, often lost, through this jumble of ravines and ridges.'[8] Clambering forwards, too tired even to duck to avoid the whistling bullets, he led his men into the teeth of the Turkish defences. He was then hit by machine-gun fire from the ridge to his right, and fell unconscious to the ground. He was lucky to survive, the bullet missing his spine by a fraction. In the four days following the landing of 9th Warwicks in the Dardanelles the battalion suffered 414 casualties. Taken from the battlefield on a bumpy stretcher and evacuated painfully by hospital ship, first to Egypt and then to England, he wrote to a friend from the Royal Victoria Hospital, Netley, where he spent six months in convalescence, that he had been 'pipped' through the lungs by a bullet that 'smashed the left shoulder to blazes and bust the top of my arm.'[9] His experience of Sari Bair – the chaos, lack of proper attention to requirements for resupply and medical care, and the appalling distance between the senior officers and the men they commanded – had a profound and long-lasting impact on the young officer new to the human agony of war. For him, the fighting man always came first. It was this fundamental principle of good leadership that Slim explained to an audience of officers of 11th East African Division on the Imphal Plain in 1944: 'I tell you, therefore, as officers, that you will neither eat, nor drink, nor sleep, nor smoke, nor even sit down until you have personally seen that your men have done those things. If you will do this for them, they will follow you to the end of the world. And, if you do not, I will break you.'

Above: Newspaper photograph of officers of 9th Battalion, Royal Warwickshire Regiment. The battalion was raised from across the West Midlands. Its first deployment was to 'Gally-poly' in early 1915. The Warwicks arrived on Cape Helles on 13 July 1915. Slim was shot through the chest, and seriously wounded, on 8 August 1915. (Ian Pearson)

---

8.  Notes in the Slim Papers, Churchill Archive, Cambridge University.

9.  Letter to Phillip Pratt, 28 August 1915, Slim Papers, Churchill Archive, Cambridge University.

The story that Slim, like Field Marshal 'Wully' Robertson, made it from the bottom of the Army all the way to the top is a myth. As a member of the OTC Slim found himself gazetted as a second lieutenant in the Royal Warwickshire Regiment on 22 August 1914. He was 23. He joined the 9th Battalion, part of Kitchener's First Army, which formed up on Salisbury Plain in September 1914. (Viscount Slim)

Above: Slim in a wadi in Mesopotamia. The 9th Battalion, part of the 13th Division, found itself in Mesopotamia after Gallipoli. Slim rejoined them at Kut-el-Amara in October 1916, and took command of his old company. Maude began to advance towards Kut in December 1917 and Baghdad fell in March 1918. (Ian Pearson)

At Gallipoli he had ended up commanding his company as a temporary second lieutenant. It was the sort of rapid battlefield elevation common in that most bloody of wars, when young officers scarcely out of training were forced by the death or wounding of their superiors to step up to command responsibility while still very inexperienced. They learned fast, or died. On return to England, he was granted a regular commission as a second lieutenant. A year later, in October 1916, fully convalesced, he rejoined his battalion, rebuilt following the arrival of drafts from England, in Mesopotamia. On 4 March 1917, he was promoted to lieutenant. He was wounded a second time in 1917, in the arm, and was awarded the Military Cross. Evacuated to India, he was given the temporary rank of major in the 6th Gurkha Rifles on 2 November 1918. He was formally promoted to captain and transferred to the Indian Army on 22 May 1919. From thenceforward until he took brigade command in 1940 his life was that of a regimental officer of 6th Gurkha Rifles. He was home. He excelled at regimental soldiering and loved his Gurkha soldiers, a rare breed of warrior whom he had first encountered on that bloody Gallipoli ridge in August 1915. His success was evidenced by his appointment as adjutant of the battalion 1921, the most important commissioned post in the battalion beside that of the commanding officer. The adjutant, as the commanding officer's staff officer, was responsible for the behaviour and discipline of all the officers, for the training of new recruits

Right: Officers' mess in Mesopotamia, 1918. Slim was wounded for the second time on 29 March 1918, when an ill-advised frontal assault nevertheless took the Turkish trenches along the Tigris north of Baghdad, but at a cost of a third of the attacking force of three battalions of 39th Brigade. Slim was wounded in the arm by a piece of enemy artillery shrapnel. (Ian Pearson)

and for the orderliness of the battalion in its day-to-day functioning. It was a post for a senior and experienced captain, with the personality and character to achieve the difficult balance of quiet, understated but obvious discipline necessary in a happy regiment. When Second Lieutenant Bruce Scott arrived in the battalion in 1922 he was struck by the quiet control Slim exerted over the battalion: 'Without being sergeant-majorish Slim, through his firm and tactful handling, kept everybody in their right place… with the result that we were a very happy crowd. He was a perfectionist – under his eye the guardmounting and bugles very quickly became as good as they had ever been; he spoke the language well, knew the men intimately and they in turn had a respect and affection for him.'

During this period Slim spent the equivalent of four years, with his battalion, on the North-west Frontier, preserving the peace against the wiles of the Tochi Wazirs. These were campaigns that emphasized individual soldiering skills, marksmanship and physical fitness, as well as the leadership and professionalism of the junior, regimental leaders. It was a crucially important proving ground for the Indian Army's junior leaders. Many of those who came to prominence in Burma during World War II cut their teeth on the North-west Frontier between the wars. A number of these were from the 6th Gurkha Rifles, whose nickname in the Indian Army was 'The Mongol Conspiracy'. In 1926 Slim was sent to the Indian Staff College at Quetta where he graduated as the top student. On 1 January 1930, he was given the brevet rank of major (a rank that did not give him regimental seniority), with formal promotion to this rank on 19 May 1933. His performance at Staff College resulted in his appointment first to Army Headquarters India in Delhi and then to Staff College, Camberley, in England, where he taught from 1934 to 1937. A fellow instructor at Camberley, Lieutenant-Colonel Archibald Nye, who was later to become Vice Chief of the Imperial General Staff, was struck by Slim's ability, regarding him to be 'probably the best all round officer of his rank in the Imperial Army. One could not fail to respect him since he had two qualities at a very high degree – quality of character which included complete integrity and at the same time the quality of a very good intellect. One does not often come across a man with both these qualities so developed.' Slim's strength, Nye believed, lay in his 'complete sanity and soundness, for he was a man who always had his feet on the ground, and he had a sense of stability, solidity and reliability.' Could, from this soundness and certainty, be found

Mesopotamia 1918. This photograph of Slim and an officer of the 9th Royal Warwicks was taken by his friend and colleague, Captain Chris Pearson, who was to be killed in 1919 when acting as a political officer with the Kurds. (Ian Pearson)

the wellsprings of genius? Nye thought so, for Slim's other characteristic was a first-class brain, which he used to think in a logical and ruthlessly analytical way. Only war, of a major kind, would put this capability to the test. Although none of them was yet to know it (although many suspected), the opportunity for that to happen was not too far distant.

In 1938, Slim was promoted to lieutenant-colonel and given command of 2nd Battalion, 7th Gurkha Rifles. On 8 June 1939, he was promoted to the temporary rank of brigadier and appointed head of the Senior Officers' School at Belgaum, India.

# WORLD WAR II, 1939–43

On the outbreak of World War II, Slim was given command of 10th Indian Infantry Brigade of the 5th Indian Infantry Division and sent to Sudan where he took part in the East African Campaign to liberate Ethiopia from the Italians. He was to learn much from this experience that was to influence him in later years. In particular, his brigade faltered during an offensive against the Italians in the area of Fort Gallabat in early November 1940, and Slim subsequently chastened himself for being insufficiently aggressive. After capturing the fort Slim failed to press his advantage immediately. The Essex Regiment had suffered 45 casualties in the attack, most of his 12 tanks had been destroyed by mines and the Italians retained command of the air. Slim, in his words, 'took counsel of his fears' and did not press on to his objective, the nearby village of Metemma. It was a mistake. Metemma had been about to surrender to the advancing British when Slim called his brigade to a halt. The Italians counterattacked heavily from the air and Slim, eager to avoid unnecessary casualties, decided to withdraw.

He was lucky to have a second chance for, as he himself admitted, he had performed poorly. In the fighting for Keren in January 1941 he was wounded in the buttocks by a strafing Italian fighter. Soon afterwards, however, he had the opportunity to rectify the failure at Gallabat.

## Syria

In June 1941 he was given the rank of acting major-general and command of the 10th Indian Infantry Division in Iraq at the closing stages of the Anglo-Iraqi War and the opening of the Syria–Lebanon Campaign. It was during the second of these campaigns that he demonstrated extraordinary qualities of resourcefulness and ingenuity, without

An unusually formal photograph of the young Captain W. J. Slim, taken when he was adjutant of 1/6th Gurkhas in 1924. Slim had the photograph taken in order to impress on the parents of the young Aileen Robertson, visiting India with her aunt in 1924 (neither of whom, of course, had ever met the penniless young Gurkha officer), that he had a respectable career and reasonable prospects! They married in Bombay on New Year's Day, 1926. (Viscount Slim)

# The extent of operations in which Slim was involved, 1940–45

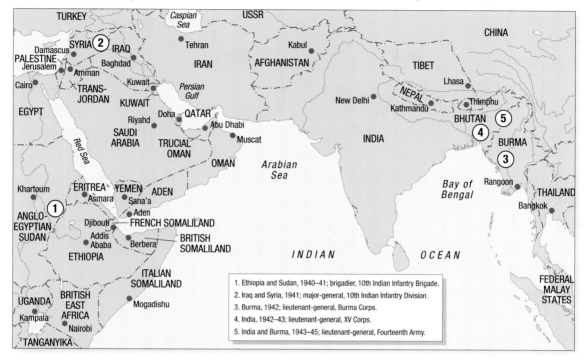

1. Ethiopia and Sudan, 1940–41; brigadier, 10th Indian Infantry Brigade.
2. Iraq and Syria, 1941; major-general, 10th Indian Infantry Division.
3. Burma, 1942; lieutenant-general, Burma Corps.
4. India, 1942–43; lieutenant-general, XV Corps.
5. India and Burma, 1943–45; lieutenant-general, Fourteenth Army.

which his plan may well have failed. Slim's division advanced into eastern Syria from Iraq in mid-June 1941 as part of a three-pronged invasion of Vichy territory designed to prevent Hitler gaining a foothold in the Middle East. Wavell's plan (he was the British Commander-in-Chief Middle East) was for Slim's division to apply pressure on Syria's eastern flank through the capture of the town of Deir-ez-Zor on the Upper Euphrates and thereafter to advance on Aleppo. The capital of Eastern Syria and a historic crossing of the Euphrates, Deir-ez-Zor was the meeting place of desert tracks that converged from across Asia Minor on the only bridge to cross the river for many hundreds of miles. The long distances combined with a lack of adequate transport for his division and the difficulties of maintaining a long line of communication for his petrol and stores, particularly in the face of regular attacks by insurgents, made any long-range penetration with substantial forces a significant challenge.

Because of these difficulties and the need to protect his supply lines while he advanced, Slim decided to advance with one brigade forwards while his other brigade guarded his

Below: Smoke rising from Fort Gallabat, Eritrea, November 1940. Slim accepted that his initial approach to the attack on this Italian-held fort was insufficiently bold and led to the failure of the attack. (IWM, E 1227)

rear. Establishing a base first at the straggling riverside village of Haditha, part-way between Habbaniya and the French border, he stocked it with supplies for 15 days. On 28 June the frontier post at Abu Kemal was captured, but the French had by that time fled. By stripping Iraq Command bare, Slim gathered some 300 3-ton trucks to assist in his advance up the Euphrates. In total his leading brigade had some 800 vehicles; the plan was to advance with these about 200 miles (320km) in two days.

The advance into Syria was extremely difficult in the intense heat and clouds of dust, made worse by the movement of such a large number of vehicles. Deir-ez-Zor was well defended by machine-gun posts and concrete gun emplacements, especially to the south and west of the town. The garrison was said to comprise between 2,000 and 4,000 troops, with up to four batteries of artillery, a desert company, Foreign Legionnaires and armoured cars. This was not a place that would fall to a conventional attack. Even if he had had a preponderance of troops, Slim was not by now disposed to tactics that would have entailed an attack from a direction the enemy would expect. Indeed, with the limited troops available to him, he was convinced that only a quick surprise attack would have any chance of success. Accordingly, a plan was hatched in which most of the forward brigade would move to the north in a conventional approach whilst at the same time a motorized column would make its way in a wide flanking move across the desert to attack the town from the rear. In the process it was hoped that the defenders would be surprised and their defence dislocated. The attack was planned for 2 July.

The plan was full of risks, however. The 80-mile (130km) approach through the desert could easily have been discovered from the air, and navigation in the desert was notoriously difficult. However, Slim was convinced that boldness was the right approach, and he was certain that with careful control his plan had every chance of success. The advance on the right flank began on 1 July and made good progress, although the column was attacked a number of times from the air. The lack of effective air defences and the paucity of supporting aircraft made the division desperately vulnerable to the unrelenting attacks by Vichy bombers flying all the way from Aleppo. However, at the end of the first day of travel the motorized column out in the desert flank had been badly dispersed by a sandstorm, attacked from the air, and had consumed more fuel than planned,

The Essex Regiment at Palmyra, Syria, 1941. The fratricidal war in Syria in 1941 saw Slim demonstrate that he had learned the fundamental lesson of Eritrea, namely that the bold step is usually always the correct one. As a result Slim's feint and hook at Deir-ez-Zor was a dramatic success, despite the huge logistical risks that his advance had entertained. To the west, in the same campaign, 1st Battalion, The Essex Regiment, helped clear Vichy forces from Palymra. The regiment's second battalion had been in Slim's brigade at Gallabat. (IWM, E 004987)

making it doubtful that it would reach the rear of Deir-ez-Zor as planned. The brigade commander ordered the column to stop. When, very early the next morning Slim discovered that his plan had gone awry, he leapt into a vehicle and drove immediately across the desert in the darkness to reach the stationary column.

Reviewing his options, Slim determined that the approach most likely to succeed, despite its risks, was his original plan, despite the overconsumption of fuel. Every way he looked at it, the desert flank option was vastly superior to the idea of mounting a frontal attack. Siphoning petrol from all vehicles not required for the operation, Slim managed to provide just enough fuel – 5,000 gallons – to enable his desert column to continue. The column emerged to the rear of Deir-ez-Zor just as planned at first light on 3 July, catching the defenders in an entirely unexpected pincer movement that determined the battle. After a day of fighting the surrounded Vichy forces surrendered. Slim's division was now free, resupplied from captured stores, to motor deep into Syria and thereby to complete the strategic squeeze which Wavell had applied against the country, and which led to its eventual collapse.

The following month Slim led his division in the four-day invasion of Persia. His experience of command was developing rapidly, and in the deftness and calmness of decisions made under the threat of imminent failure he made an immediate impression on his superiors. He was twice mentioned in dispatches during 1941 and received the Distinguished Service Order for his victory at Deir-ez-Zor.

## Burma

Slim was thrown into the maelstrom of Burma on 8 March 1942. The Japanese attack on South-east Asia had begun the previous December, simultaneous with the attack on Pearl Harbor. By February the Japanese had captured Rangoon, sweeping the weak and unprepared British forces before them. General Sir Harold Alexander commanded the Burma Army, having arrived as Rangoon fell, and weeks later he was provided with a corps commander – Slim (rapidly promoted to the rank of lieutenant-general) – to command the two weak divisions that remained. The 17th Indian Division had lost much of its strength at the Sittang River, while 1st Burma Division was made up mainly of paramilitary troops not trained or equipped to take on a first-class enemy. The one real blessing he possessed was 7th Armoured Brigade,

At Yenangyaung in April 1942 British troops destroy equipment and machinery at the oilfields during the retreat from Burma. Slim's cool-headedness during the retreat, in command of the fighting troops within the Burma Army (Burma Corps), played a singular role in the success of the fighting withdrawal to India. (IWM, IND 989)

also newly arrived, with their Stuart light tanks and battle experience from North Africa.

Slim was determined to fight, but it very quickly became clear that the Japanese held virtually every advantage. They moved fast, were well led and had command of the sky. The country was in turmoil, with refugees blocking the roads, and the Japanese could outflank defensive positions prepared by the British almost at will. It quickly became clear that a fighting retreat back to Indian Manipur was the only thing that could save what troops remained and prevent another humiliation like Singapore. Slim planned and commanded this withdrawal with calm brilliance. When, in late May, Slim's Burma Corps straggled across the Chindwin and over the hills into Manipur, they undoubtedly looked like a rabble after their 100-day, 1,000-mile (1,600km) fighting withdrawal. But they remained soldiers nevertheless, disciplined and loyal despite their rags and exhaustion. Morale, despite some bitter blows, remained strong. Despite the humiliation and bitterness of defeat, Burma Corps had not collapsed or surrendered, and for the most part had held together under the most trying circumstances imaginable. Units, though exhausted, had fought well, with some notable tactical successes against the pursuing Japanese. 'We brought our weapons out with us, and we carried our wounded, too' Slim recalled. 'Dog-tired soldiers, hardly able to put one foot in front of another, would stagger along for hours carrying or holding up a wounded comrade.... In those days, if anyone had gone to me with a single piece of good news I would have

### Corps commander's orders group, Yenangyaung, 18 April 1942

The withdrawal of 1st Burma Division (part of Slim's Burma Corps) into the Yenangyaung pocket over the period 17 and 19 April 1942 during the retreat to India was the severest trial yet faced by Slim's troops. It turned out not to be a battle for the oilfields, as these had already been destroyed, but rather a battle for the survival of 1st Burma Division. The intense heat and the lack of water provided the most pressing physical trials. There was virtually no fresh water as the east bank of the Irrawaddy, the only source of water, was now in Japanese hands. It was crucial that his friend, Major-General Bruce Scott held on for as long as he could. Slim realized that with no reserve of his own, Scott's only hope of relief lay in assistance from the Chinese. He was given the 38th Chinese Division, commanded by one of Chiang Kai-shek's ablest commanders, Major-General Sun Li Jen. Slim rated Sun highly. Taking a considerable risk Slim placed all his available tanks and artillery under Sun's direct command. It was a masterly piece of diplomacy and worked remarkably well. But it was not simply good politics; unity of command for all forces involved in the battle required a single commander and a clear, unambiguous chain of command. Here Slim (1) briefs Brigadier Anstice (2) of the 7th Armoured Brigade and Major-General Sun Li Jen (3). The truck on which Slim's map is pinned belongs to 2 RTR, as does the Stuart light tank (4) in the background. Brigadier Taffy Davies (5), Slim's loyal and effective chief of staff, stands behind the corps commander. The Yenangyaung counterattack proved to be successful, allowing the withdrawal to continue.

burst out crying. Nobody ever did.' As the Official British Historian asserts, 'the Army in Burma, without once losing its cohesion, had retreated nearly one thousand miles in some three and a half months – the longest retreat ever carried out by a British Army – and for the last seven hundred miles had virtually carried its base with it.'[10]

Slim, however, refused to take the credit for the performance of Burma Corps, attributing the men's morale in part to his generals, both part of the 'Mongol Conspiracy' from 6th Gurkha Rifles, Major-Generals 'Punch' Cowan and Bruce Scott. The retreat had been a hard lesson in the fundamentals of leadership, and the experience reinforced Slim's determination thereafter to ensure that his men were commanded by the best leaders he could gather around him.

Slim had ample opportunity after he had relinquished his command of Burma Corps to consider why the imperial army had been so humiliated in Burma. In *Defeat into Victory* he considered the issues of lack of preparation, the lack of any viable land communications between India and Burma, the smallness and unsuitability of the forces in Burma at the time of the Japanese invasion, the inadequacy of the air forces available to him, the hostility of some of the local population, the 'extreme inefficiency of the whole intelligence system' and the lack of training of the Burma Army. Two factors in particular, however, he considered to have been critical determinants in the defeat.

The first was that 'we had taken a thorough beating. We, the Allies, had been outmanoeuvred, outfought and outgeneralled.' Japanese commanders were 'confident, bold to the point of foolhardiness, and so aggressive that never for one day did they lose the initiative'. By contrast Allied generals were slow to grasp the potential for decisive and aggressive action and consistently underestimated the ability of the Japanese to achieve what the British would consider impossible in the jungle. Commanders as a whole lacked vision, single-mindedness and the moral and mental robustness necessary to withstand the succession of shocks delivered by the Japanese. The Allies appeared constantly to be wrong-footed. Slim's comments regarding generalship included, of course, his own performance. 'For myself' he comments, 'I had little to be proud of: I could not rate my generalship high. The only test of generalship is success, and I had succeeded in nothing I had attempted.' Although Slim was remarkably – perhaps excessively – self-critical, his criticisms were directed at the broadest spectrum of senior leadership concerned with the campaign, from top to bottom.

The second significant British failing in 1942, Slim believed, lay in the dramatic inferiority of British tactics. Relative to the innovation and imagination apparent in the Japanese approach to war the Allies had been completely outclassed. 'The Japanese could – and did – do many things that we could not' Slim wrote. 'The chief of these and the tactical method

---

10. Stanley Woodburn Kirby *The War Against Japan,* Volume II (London: HMSO, 1958), p. 210.

on which all their success were based was the "hook".... Time and again the Japanese used these tactics, more often than not successfully, until our troops and commanders began to acquire a road-block mentality which often developed into an inferiority complex.' The 'hook' was merely a classic 'turning' movement; that many units in Burma Corps were unable to counter this relatively simple tactical device testified to their profound lack of confidence in dealing with an aggressive and inventive enemy. The power of the 'hook' lay in the psychological dislocation brought about by the awful sensation of being trapped, which to inexperienced troops could be devastating. The inability to counter these tactics in 1942 allowed the Japanese to retain the initiative on the battlefield.

Slim, with his daughter Una in India, 1943. His son, John, joined the 6th Gurkha Rifles in 1944 and served in Burma for the remainder of the war. (Getty, 3276432)

The retreat was a valuable learning experience for Slim. The unknown divisional commander from the military backwaters of Iraq had proved his considerable abilities under the most trying of circumstances. Indeed, it could be argued that the retreat to India was the greatest test of his leadership, even more than the long, hard battles against the Japanese that lay ahead. Throughout the severest trial he exhibited a constant, calm and unruffled professionalism.

He had proved two things. First, that he was able to plan, organize and command in circumstances of overwhelming crisis. The campaign had marked him out as a commander of considerable mental stamina, a man who was tough and tenacious in the face of almost overwhelming adversity, and who refused to give up when all the facts seemed to indicate that there was no hope for his bedraggled and defeated forces. Second, he had proved that he could keep his head and display quite remarkable resilience and imperturbability when the military situation appeared irretrievable. Even after a succession of lost battles his composure made a dramatic and decisive impact on his men. Major Michael Calvert, recalled watching Slim during the hot, dusty days of the withdrawal, the corps commander presenting 'an indomitable and unshaken front in the face of these disasters, and his rather ponderous jokes cheered his staff and commanders when they were at their lowest ebb.... [He] was stubborn' Calvert wrote, 'he had an indomitable spirit and, like the British troops, he never knew when he was beaten.'[11] When the 26-year-old Major Ian Lyall Grant met him during the second week of April 1942 with only six weeks of the retreat from Burma left to run, he was, despite the otherwise apparent hopelessness of the situation, buoyed up by Slim's calm reassurance that the situation, although bleak, was under control. After listening to Slim brief them, he and his fellows felt for the first time

11. Michael Calvert *Slim* (London: Ballantine, 1973), p. 31.

19

# The retreat from Burma

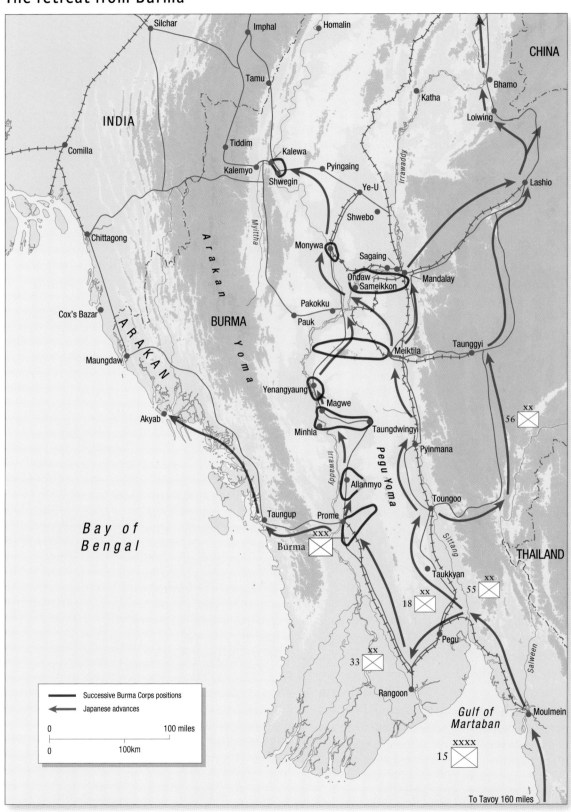

CHINA

INDIA

Silchar
Imphal
Homalin
Tamu
Bhamo
Katha
Loiwing
Comilla
Tiddim
Kalewa
Pyingaing
Lashio
Kalemyo
Ye-U
Shwegin
Shwebo
Chittagong
Monywa
Sagaing
Mandalay
Cox's Bazar
Ondaw
Sameikkon
Pakokku
Maungdaw
Pauk
Meiktila
Taunggyi
Akyab
BURMA
Yenangyaung
Magwe
Minhla
Taungdwingyi
56
Pyinmana
Allanmyo
Toungoo
THAILAND
Taungup
Prome
Burma
Taukkyan
55
18
Pegu
33
Rangoon
Gulf of
Martaban
Moulmein
15

*Bay of*
*Bengal*

A r a k a n
A R A K A N
B u r m a   y o m a
P e g u   Y o m a
Myittha
Irrawaddy
Irrawaddy
Sittang
Salween

Successive Burma Corps positions
Japanese advances

0 ————————— 100 miles
0 ————————— 100km

To Tavoy 160 miles

that they 'now had a leader who realized that new methods were required to counter Japanese tactics and was prepared to think them out.'[12]

His men, too, had no doubt who was responsible for bringing them out of Burma. As Slim said farewell to his troops in the days before his departure from Imphal on 20 May he received an accolade reserved only for the likes of a Napoleon or a Wellington: his troops cheered him. 'To be cheered by troops whom you have led to victory is grand and exhilarating' he commented. 'To be cheered by the gaunt remnants of those whom you have led only in defeat, withdrawal and disaster, is infinitely moving – and humbling.' Some vestiges of victory, Slim believed, could be drawn from defeat.

After the retreat from Burma he was given command of XV Corps, but fell out with his unsympathetic and deeply conservative army commander, Lieutenant-General Noel Irwin. A disastrous British offensive against Japanese-held Arakan between late 1942 and May 1943, designed and overseen by Irwin, left the ill-trained and badly led British forces reeling from another serious defeat, in which Slim had but a peripheral role. All the while, however, he was formulating his plans, developing his ideas and training the men of his corps to take on the Japanese and win. Irwin's warped personality led him to attempt to blame Slim for the disaster in Arakan, and he tried to sack him. This perfidy was transparent to Wavell, now the Commander-in-Chief India, however, and Irwin himself was removed. Irwin at least had the manners to send a signal to Slim: 'You're not sacked, I am'. Slim was promoted to Irwin's job and given the opportunity no British soldier had been given since the days of Wellington: the chance to train an army from scratch and single-handedly mould it into something of his own making.

# INDIA AND BURMA, 1943–45

## Rebuilding an army

The British/Indian Army in Burma in 1945 was a considerably different one to that which had retreated from the country in 1942. A significant reason for this was the work that Slim undertook, first as the commander of XV Corps in 1942 and the whole of Fourteenth Army following his promotion in August 1943, to transform the way the army fought, especially the quality of its leaders, the suitability of its tactics and its physical and mental toughness.

If one thing was abundantly clear to Slim after the retreat it was the necessity for realistic, imaginative and demanding training, both at the individual level and at that of the unit – section, platoon, company and battalion. When he took command of XV Corps in June 1942 he introduced a punishing programme of training that embraced every soldier in every

---

12. Ian Lyall Grant and Kazuo Tamayama *Burma 1942: The Japanese Invasion. Both Sides Tell the Story of a Savage Jungle War* (Chichester: The Zampi Press, 1999), p. 233.

A DC3 dropping supplies over Arakan November 1944. Air transport and aerial resupply were innovations developed strongly by Slim to counteract the tyrannies of geography and distance in the Far East. The use of aircraft in Fourteenth Army became a fundamental part of the entire approach to war, and the land and air forces an integrated entity. (IWM, SE 2622)

type of unit. Physical toughening, weapon training and practice at cross-country mobility with mules was carried out despite the monsoon rains. Endurance marches, river crossings, patrolling, night training, field discipline and mock battles with live ammunition, mortars and artillery in all weathers became the norm, and were rehearsed constantly.

Slim drafted a summary of the key tactical ideas that had impressed him in Burma, some of which were lessons learned directly from the Japanese, which he then promulgated to his corps. His aim was to devise clear and simple strategies for defeating the Japanese and in so doing started from first principles.

1. The individual soldier must learn, by living, moving and exercising in it, that the jungle is neither impenetrable nor unfriendly. When he has once learned to move and live in it, he can use it for concealment, covered movement and surprise.
2. Patrolling is the master key to jungle fighting. All units, not only infantry battalions, must learn to patrol in the jungle, boldly, widely, cunningly and offensively.
3. All units must get used to having Japanese parties in their rear, and, when this happens, regard not themselves, but the Japanese, as 'surrounded'.
4. In defence, no attempt should be made to hold long continuous lines. Avenues of approach must be covered and enemy penetration between our posts dealt with at once by mobile local reserves who have completely reconnoitred the country.
5. There should rarely be frontal attacks and never frontal attacks on narrow fronts. Attacks should follow hooks and come in from flank or rear, while pressure holds the enemy in front.
6. Tanks can be used in almost any country except swamp. In close country they must always have infantry with them to defend and reconnoitre for them. They should always be used in the maximum numbers available and capable of being deployed. Whenever possible penny packets must be avoided. 'The more you use, the fewer you lose.'
7. There are no non-combatants in jungle warfare. Every unit and sub-unit, including medical ones, is responsible for its own all-round protection, including patrolling, at all times.
8. If the Japanese are allowed to hold the initiative they are formidable. When we have it, they are confused and easy to kill. By mobility away from roads, surprise and offensive action we must regain and keep the initiative.

These principles outlined the key requirements necessary to enable the individual soldier to master the art of fighting in the jungle against a skilful, determined and resourceful opponent by day and night. Training was central to the discipline soldiers needed to control their fear, and that of their subordinates, in battle; to allow them to think clearly and shoot straight in a crisis, and to inspire them to maximum physical and mental endeavour. Slim recognized that the psychological dimension of battle against the Japanese was formidable. The Japanese were not bogeymen, as many in Burma Corps had realized during the retreat, but the myth of their invincibility had swept the British Indian Army following the unprecedented disasters of the loss of Malaya, Singapore and Burma. The Japanese soldier was, nevertheless, well trained and hardy, prepared to accept almost any hardship and sacrifice. They coordinated artillery, armour and air support well with attacks by infantry; their camouflage and concealment was excellent and they made the maximum psychological impact through their tactics of surprise.

Slim's aim was to train the Army ruthlessly to live by these new standards. His tough training regime in XV Corps was in time extended to the remainder of Eastern Army (which became, in August 1943, Fourteenth Army). Training schools were set up across eastern India to train infantry in the battle skills they would need to fight the Japanese. Signals, engineer and artillery courses blossomed, as did Army/Air Force air-to-ground cooperation courses, infantry and tank cooperation training, mule handling courses, parachute, air landing and glider training, and innumerable other courses and instruction dealing with everything from the provision of air-dropped supplies to the proper crossing of rivers. 'Our training grew more ambitious' Slim recalled, 'until we were staging inter-divisional exercises over wide ranges of country under tough conditions. Units lived for weeks on end in the jungle and learnt its ways. We hoped we had finally dispelled the fatal idea that the Japanese had something we had not.'

One consequence of this intensive training was the removal and replacement of commanders at all levels who proved unable to cope with the pace and pressures of his regime. In particular, Slim ensured that those who were yet untried in the rigours of this type of fighting proved themselves before taking over command by understudying their jobs first. It would have been unfair, he argued, 'either to the men they were to command or to the officers themselves to have thrust them raw into a jungle battle.' Most won their spurs '… but some did not. It was as well to find out first.'

While relentless training was one of Slim's remedies for the state of the army he inherited in 1943, this itself spoke of a far deeper analysis Slim had made into how best to motivate his army to fight and defeat the Japanese in battle. By October 1943 he had developed a plan of action to rebuild the

Examining a captured Japanese sword with a Gurkha of 17th Indian Division (the Black Cats) on 31 December 1943. Slim first met the Gurkhas at Gallipoli in 1915 and joined them in 1921. He was to write many years later: 'The Almighty created in the Gurkha an ideal infantryman, indeed an ideal rifleman, brave, tough, patient, adaptable, skilled in field-craft, intensely proud of his military record and unswervingly loyal.' (Getty, 3038194)

Slim together with Air Vice Marshal Vincent (AOC 221 Group) and Major-General H. M. Chambers, GOC 26th Indian Division, at Government House in Rangoon, 8 May 1945. Victory was sweet. (IWM, SE 4046)

fighting spirit of his troops based on three principles of action. These dealt with spiritual, intellectual and material factors in turn.

By the 'spiritual' principle he meant that the Army must be a great and noble object, its achievement must be vital, the method of achievement must be active and aggressive and each man must feel that what he is and what he does matters directly towards the attainment of the object. It was critical, he argued, that all troops, of whatever rank, background and nationality, believed in the cause they were fighting for. The cause itself had to be just. In Burma, Slim wrote, 'We fought for the clean, the decent, the free things of life…. We fought only because the powers of evil had attacked these things.'

By the 'intellectual' principle he meant that soldiers had to be convinced that the object could be attained. The principal task was to destroy the notion that the Japanese soldier was invincible. Equally, the soldier had also to know that the organization to which he belonged was an efficient one. He knew that the physical care of a soldier in the field has a direct bearing on his performance in battle: lack of food, water, medical support or contact with home works to weaken the resolve, over time, of even the stoutest man. By the 'material' foundation Slim meant that each man had to feel that he would get a fair deal from his commanders and from the Army generally, that he would, as far as humanly possible, be given the best weapons and equipment for his task and that his living and working conditions would be made as good as they could be.

## 15th Division fighting in the Mayu Range, Arakan, February 1944

The fighting in Arakan from February 1944 saw the Japanese superiority on the battlefield disappear. After a disastrous first campaign in Arakan in late 1942 and early 1943 Slim began retraining his army. The essential requirement, in combat and support units alike, was for well-trained, motivated and confident troops. Units that were able to infiltrate through and around Japanese positions at night, separated from their regular supply chain, and able to form quick defensive 'boxes' when threatened in turn by Japanese infiltration, needed to be exceptionally confident in their fighting skills, their tactics and their leaders. Such could be achieved only as the result of hard and realistic training. Even administrative and support units had to be able to stand fast in the event of encirclement and defend their perimeter against attack. Under rigorous new leadership new life began to cascade through the veins of what was shortly to become Fourteenth Army. Every man was rigorously trained as a fighter. Live training with artillery, mortars and medium machine guns was carried out. All ranks practised fighting with tanks, artillery, mortars and aircraft as well as bayonet and grenade. Confidence returned, and when it came, the Japanese offensive in Arakan was decisively repelled.

Slim's Fourteenth Army was polyglot. Here, troops of the 11th East African Division on the road to Kalewa, Burma, during the Chindwin River crossing in late 1944. (IWM, SE 1884)

## Imphal and Kohima

When, as the new commander of Fourteenth Army, Slim considered his prospects in late 1943 for defeating the Japanese in Burma, he knew that his task would be made infinitely easier if the Japanese advanced into India first. The 'March on Delhi', loudly trumpeted by 'Tokyo Rose' over the airwaves, provided exactly the situation Slim wanted. Instead of taking his still inexperienced army into Burma, there to fight a decisive battle against the Japanese on ground of their own choosing and where they would be strongest, he reasoned that he had a very strong chance of destroying a Japanese offensive were they to be enticed to attack Manipur. There the roles would be reversed. Experience had taught him that if they attacked into India they would do so on the flimsiest of supply arrangements, and that Japanese commanders would display fanatical determination to succeed, even if it meant suffering large numbers of casualties. Being able to defeat a Japanese thrust against Imphal would then make any subsequent attack into Burma immeasurably easier.

A scene of devastation at Naga village near Kohima taken after fierce fighting against the Japanese in April–June 1944. It was at the mountain village of Kohima, India's Thermopylae, that the Japanese invasion of India in 1944 was stopped after three months of fierce fighting. (IWM, IND 3709)

By the start of 1944 Slim knew that an attack into Assam was precisely what the Japanese intended. The plan he developed was to lure the Japanese into a decisive killing ground in the great half-circle of jungle-clad mountains facing east from Imphal. There he would lock the enemy into a close battle in which superior British firepower combined with Japanese blind tenacity – and hugely

overextended supply lines – would destroy the enemy utterly. This was a stratagem that not everyone fully understood or accepted. In particular, it entailed an acceptance of a significant Japanese advance into Assam. While Slim believed (and Mountbatten – the new commander of South East Asia Command – accepted) that this would be the undoing of the Japanese, there were many who believed that such a defensive strategy was wrong, and that Slim needed to be much more offensive.

The first opportunity Slim had to demonstrate his rebuilt army was in early 1944 in northern Arakan, against which lapped the Bay of Bengal. In preparation Slim's newly trained troops had been trained to be less reliant on the road, and more reliant on mule and, where it was necessary, air transport. If they were cut off by the Japanese, they were to regard the Japanese to be surrounded, not themselves, and to stand firm in defensive 'boxes'. Slim's plan was to then hold tight within the 'box', defend it by aggressive patrolling, support it by air, and allow the enemy to smash itself to pieces against its walls. It worked, spectacularly. In January a cautious British advance was met by a Japanese counteroffensive, a strategic feint for an offensive aimed at Manipur in mid-March. The 7th Indian Infantry Division was quickly surrounded along with parts of the 5th Indian Infantry Division. The 7th Indian Division's defence was concentrated on a number of defensive 'boxes', including the famous 'Admin Box' at Sinzweya, formed initially from supply and support troops such as drivers, cooks and mule handlers. Slim had prepared the air resupply organization to meet the demands of the impending battle. Ten days' supplies for 40,000 men were made ready for dropping. 'The complete maintenance of over a division for several days' wrote Slim, 'everything that it would require, from pills to projectiles, from bully beef to boots, was laid out, packed for dropping, at the airstrips.' This ferocious battle played a central role in proving the validity of Slim's new tactics. The fatal flaw in Japanese planning was the now-dubious assumption that they could live off captured British stores. Battering themselves repeatedly against the solid 7th Indian Division defences, the Japanese 55th Division exhausted itself and failed to capture the stores they needed to continue fighting. To their surprise the British refused to budge. Nor could they break the British-Indian lines. The Japanese were decisively defeated, withdrawing in disarray before the end of February, losing over 70 per cent of their strength in the process. Of the 7,000 Japanese who had begun the operation 'over five thousand bodies were found and counted, many more lay undiscovered in the jungle; hundreds died of exhaustion before

With General Stopford, Imphal 1944. This still, taken from a short film covering the battles of Kohima and Imphal, shows Lieutenant-General Sir Montagu Stopford following Slim, with an unidentified officer leading the party. Slim surrounded himself with fighting generals. Stopford commanded XXXIII Corps at Kohima (2nd and 7th Indian Divisions) and was chosen by Slim to lead, with Frank Messervy, the phenomenally successful advance into Burma in late 1944 and early 1945. (IWM, Film)

# The Second Arakan campaign

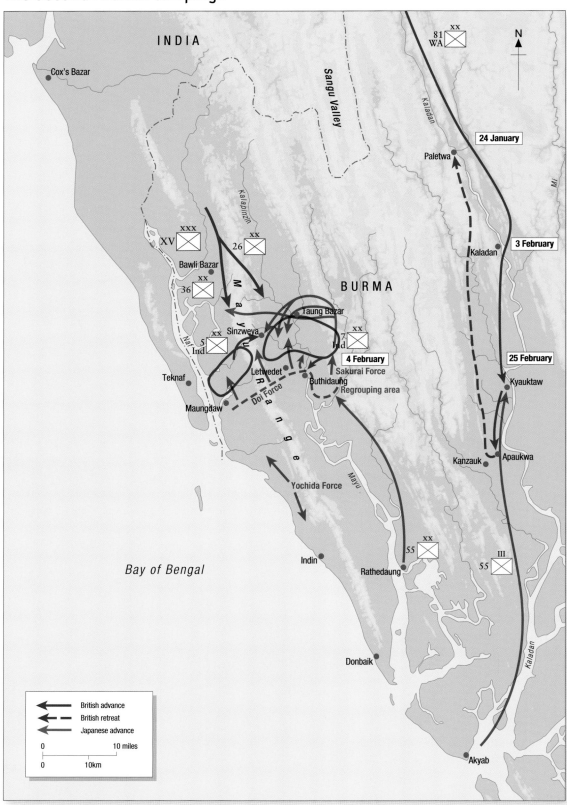

# Imphal and Kohima

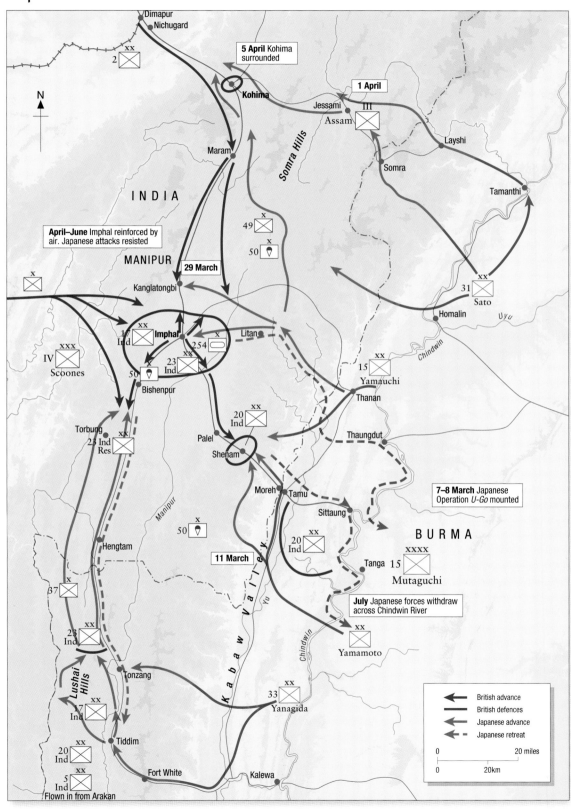

Dimapur
Nichugard

XX
2

**5 April** Kohima surrounded

**1 April**

Kohima

Jessami
Assam

III

Layshi

N

Somra

Tamanthi

Maram

Somra Hills

INDIA

49  X

50  X

**April–June** Imphal reinforced by air. Japanese attacks resisted

MANIPUR

**29 March**

XX
31  Sato

Homalin

Uyu

Kanglatongbi

X

Litan

Chindwin

17 Ind  XX  **Imphal**

IV  XXX
Scoones

254  X

15  XX
Yamauchi

50  X

23 Ind  XX

Bishenpur

Thanan

20 Ind  XX

Torbung

23 Ind Res  XX

Palel

Shenam

Thaungdut

Moreh  Tamu

**7–8 March** Japanese Operation *U-Go* mounted

Manipur

50  X

Sittaung

BURMA

Hengtam

**11 March**

20 Ind  XX

Tanga  15  XXXX
Mutaguchi

Kabaw Valley

Yu

**July** Japanese forces withdraw across Chindwin River

37  X

Chindwin

20 Ind  XX
Yamamoto

23 Ind  XX

Lushai Hills

Tonzang

33  XX
Yanagida

17 Ind  XX

Tiddim

20 Ind  XX

5 Ind  XX
Flown in from Arakan

Fort White

Kalewa

→ British advance
— British defences
→ Japanese advance
⇢ Japanese retreat

0 ——— 20 miles
0 ——— 20km

Talking to a Gurkha near Palel, Imphal, in November 1944. Sir Max Hastings has observed: 'In contrast to almost every other outstanding commander of the war, Slim was a disarmingly normal human being, possessed of notable self-knowledge. He was without pretension, devoted to his wife, Aileen, their family and the Indian Army. His calm, robust style of leadership and concern for the interests of his men won the admiration of all who served under him.... His blunt honesty, lack of bombast and unwillingness to play courtier did him few favours in the corridors of power. Only his soldiers never wavered in their devotion.' (IWM, SE 2952)

they reached safety; few survived.' The battle was, in Slim's words, a turning point, as 'For the first time a British force had met, held and decisively defeated a major Japanese attack.' The linchpin of 7th Indian Division's ability to fight was the successful utilization of air transport in an operation that proved the validity of Slim's plans for Imphal. British morale received an immediate boost.

The second test was his outstanding defeat of the Japanese 'March on Delhi', their invasion of India (Operation *C*) in 1944, which centred on the climactic battles for Imphal and Kohima. To meet this threat Slim airlifted both 5th and 7th Indian Divisions from the Arakan battlefield straight into the fray at Kohima (flying into Dimapur) and Imphal. When Lieutenant-General Mutaguchi Renya's Fifteenth Army advanced in four separate columns into Manipur, Slim withdrew his forces into the hills surrounding the Imphal Plain. The Japanese made desperate efforts to seize their objectives; Kohima, with a British garrison of 1,500, less than half of whom were trained fighting soldiers, was attacked by a division in early April. Surrounded and slowly forced back onto a single hill they were supplied by air until relief came on 20 April. The Japanese plan entailed attacking Imphal from north, east and south. The battles for Imphal and Kohima settled down to a bloody hand-to-hand struggle as the Japanese tried to gain the foothold necessary for their survival. They travelled lightly, and reserves were soon exhausted and further supplies were almost non-existent. Just as the air situation was becoming critical for Slim through poor weather and shortages of aircraft, the relieving division from Kohima began fighting its way towards Imphal, and the four beleaguered divisions began to push out from the Imphal pocket. By 22 June, the British 2nd Division from Kohima and 5th Indian Division from Imphal met north of Imphal and the road to the plain was open. The struggle for possession of the gateway to India lasted into May and mopping-up operations lasted well into July. The Japanese lost 53,500 battle casualties of the 84,300 men that had begun the offensive: Fourteenth Army suffered nearly 17,000 casualties; a quarter of which were sustained at Kohima.

## The Chindits

While Mutaguchi and Slim struggled for dominance in the bloody battles of Imphal and Kohima, Major-General Orde Wingate launched his second Chindit offensive into the heart of Burma. In August 1943 Churchill and Roosevelt had given Wingate a force of 23 infantry battalions and a vast American-supplied air armada to mount an operation into Burma in 1944. The propaganda following his first expedition in 1943 (Operation *Longcloth*), together with Churchill's flattery and support, had led Wingate to believe that he had come up with a winning strategy to defeat the Japanese.

His idea was to fly a powerful army into the heart of Japanese-held Burma, there to destroy the Japanese from within. The concept centred upon the creation by the Chindit force of strongholds capable of self-defence, in areas inaccessible to Japanese armour and artillery, to provide bases for guerrilla raids against the Japanese lines of communication supporting their offensive against Stilwell's Chinese in the far north of Burma. They would be properly garrisoned and would contain an airstrip so that supplies could be flown in and casualties flown out, as well as ground and anti-aircraft artillery, the lack of which had proved to be a severe deficiency during Operation *Longcloth*.

Wingate considered that the greatest benefit of this plan was that it would avoid the perils of a ground offensive across the Chindwin. Although a remarkable and inspiring battlefield commander, he was not a strategist, and Slim was convinced that Wingate's conception was dangerously flawed. Nevertheless, for a short period of time in late 1943 and early 1944 Wingate's ideas formed a competing strategic idea for the defeat of the Japanese in Burma. Churchill, taken by Wingate's enthusiasm, told his personal Chief of Staff, General Sir Hastings Ismay on 24 July 1943 that he considered that 'Wingate should command the Army against Burma [as he was] a man of genius and audacity'.[13]

Wingate had become fixated with the idea that his Chindit force alone would bring about the defeat of the Japanese in Burma, going so far as to doubt whether conventional forces even had a role in a future campaign. On 10 February 1944 he told Mountbatten that Fourteenth Army could never hope to be in a position to fight over the mountains bordering the Chindwin and that only the Chindits had the training and wherewithal to take the war to the Japanese in Burma. This was an unfortunate prediction, as Slim was only months away from doing precisely this with well-trained conventional troops. Further, Wingate believed that long-range penetration formations like the Chindits 'would supersede conventional formations with such impedimenta as tanks, artillery and motorised transport.' He argued that the seizure of a town in central Burma by long-range penetration forces should be the first of a series of stepping stones that could take the Allies directly to Bangkok, Saigon and thence up the coast of China. When the Chindits had seized one stepping stone they could then be consolidated by conventional divisions following up behind.

Slim and Wingate. The awkwardness between the two men is apparent in this photograph, probably taken at Lalaghat airfield in Assam on 5 March 1944 before the fly-out of the Chindits on Operation *Thursday*. Slim disapproved of Wingate's strategic fantasies, but nevertheless supported wholeheartedly the operations with which he was charged. (IWM HU 70592)

13. Churchill to Ismay, 24 July 1943. National Archives, Kew. File PREM 3, 143/8.

Slim was convinced that whilst long-range penetration operations were worthwhile, they were so only when supporting activities by conventional forces, and had little value in and of themselves. His view was that raids, no matter how spectacular, could not win wars. The problem with Wingate's strategy, so far as Slim could observe, was that it played directly to the enemy's strengths, rather than his weaknesses. Wingate's idea would have meant placing his forces precisely where the Japanese were strongest and where his own line of communication would be by air and thus extremely tenuous. By placing his force in the heart of the enemy's own territory, where the advantage of communication and supply lay firmly with the Japanese, Slim knew that Wingate could never hope to achieve the decisive advantage he sought. His aircraft-supplied troops, light in artillery and bereft of armour, would exhaust themselves quickly, particularly if they were used for conventional rather than guerrilla purposes. It would be far better, Slim reasoned, to force the Japanese into this situation of vulnerability instead.

Nevertheless, Churchill allowed Wingate his chance, and Operation *Thursday* began in early March 1944. While one unfortunate brigade had to march some 360 miles (580km) from Ledo in early February 1944 to its stronghold 27 miles (43km) north-west of Indaw, the other two brigades flew to strongholds in the Indaw area. The plan was that after two to three months

### Major Henchman and members of No. 76 Column, 23rd (Chindit) Brigade at Tseminyu in the Naga Hills, April 1944

Slim was responsible for allocating one of Orde Wingate's Chindit brigades to the mountainous northern flank of the Kohima position in March 1944, to counter Japanese moves to dominate the Naga villages and use the hill tracks to make their way down into the Brahmaputra Valley. Brigadier Lancelot Perowne's 23rd Brigade was chosen for this purpose. Divided into a number of independent columns, all sustained by airdrop from faithful Dakotas flying in from Assam, the Chindits had to fight hard to eject the Japanese from the hilltop Naga villages. This painting represents a short, one-sided fight that took place at the village of Tseminyu, two days' march due north of Kohima in April 1942, where a Japanese foraging party had taken up residence in the village within a few days of the attack beginning on Kohima. The village, perched as with all Naga villages 4,600ft (1,400m) up on the top of a steeply sided mountain peak, served as the local store for the rice the Japanese were filching from villages in the area. The approach of 76 Column, on 14 April, came as an unexpected surprise. In the dead of night, guided by a local Rengma Naga, a party of men under the command of the giant, bearded Major Henchman of 2nd Battalion, Duke of Wellington's Regiment – whose daytime attire extended to a bush hat, shorts, boots and a webbing belt holding a .38 revolver (he never seemed to wear a shirt) – climbed quietly to the summit. Unforgivably, the Japanese sentry was fast asleep. Quietly removing the man's rifle, the Japanese was knocked unconscious with a rifle butt and taken prisoner. Henchman then ascertained that the remainder of the Japanese were asleep in the hut normally reserved in the village for visiting government officials. Grenades and the rapid staccato fire of Sten sub-machine guns surprised the sleeping tenants and in a short while the very one-sided battle was over.

A railway bridge behind Japanese lines is blown up by Chindits. Slim disagreed with Wingate's principal strategic philosophy, namely that the war could be won by inserting forces in the Japanese rear, there to 'gnaw at his vitals'. Instead, Slim argued that the best strategy was to draw the enemy into killing fields of his own making, where the Japanese would be at a logistical disadvantage, and where the British could 'come at him from land and air.' The complete destruction of Mutaguchi's Operation *C* by August 1944 demonstrated the fundamental correctness of Slim's approach to war. (IWM, SE 7924)

these brigades would be replaced *in situ* by the three relief brigades. The expedition started well, and the fly-in was a considerable success. Over the first four nights, 272 aircraft landed at the 'Broadway' stronghold with no interference from the Japanese and within a week 9,000 men, 1,350 animals and 250 tons of stores, an anti-aircraft and a 25-pdr gun battery, had been landed by 650 Dakota and glider sorties into the heart of Burma. This gave Wingate 12,000 men well placed as he put it, 'in the enemy's guts'. There was very little interference from the Japanese air force, which had been reduced by this time to approximately 90 aircraft in the whole of Burma. Surprise low-level air attacks were made on a number of enemy airfields that further reduced the Japanese ability to counter allied activity both in the air and on the ground over the period of the fly-in. During the remainder of the month, and in April, Wingate's force mounted attacks throughout the area, cutting the railway to Myitkyina, and dominating a 30-mile-long (48km) corridor astride the railway.

The landings took the Japanese by surprise. The first news of the landings reached Mutaguchi's Fifteenth Army Headquarters on 9 March, but it took some time for the size and significance of the invasion to sink in. Nevertheless, once this had been appreciated within four weeks a force of divisional size was formed to counter the landings. When in place, Slim agreed to Wingate's plan to divert a brigade of Chindits to attack Mutaguchi's lines of communication that stretched across the Chindwin and into India in support of Operation *C*.

Wingate believed that Chindit action would degrade Mutaguchi's supply lines to such an extent that it would be the decisive factor in bringing about the defeat of Fifteenth Army. When this had been proved, as he was sure it would be, Wingate believed that his small army would be substantially reinforced and perhaps even given the lead in defeating the Japanese. The flaw in this logic was that Mutaguchi had taken so many logistical risks that Fifteenth Army proved almost entirely resilient to attacks on its supply line, and assaults on it in the early weeks of an offensive therefore had a marginal impact on Japanese plans.

Three weeks after the initial fly-in Wingate was killed in an air crash in the hills west of Imphal and as a consequence the nature of the operation changed immediately. 'Without his presence to animate it', wrote Slim, 'Special Force would no longer be the same to others or to itself. He had created, inspired, defended it and given it confidence; it was the offspring of his vivid imagination and ruthless energy. It had no other parent.' It is impossible not to conclude that Operation *Thursday* was the product not of strategic necessity but of the determined promotion of one man. With his death, the idea evaporated and the whole exercise, despite the enormous commitment and sacrifice of the men involved, became a strategic sideshow.

As it happened, the smashing of Fifteenth Army against the rocks of Imphal and Kohima between March and June 1944 entirely vindicated Slim's strategy and rendered nugatory Wingate's competing view. A retrained and revitalized Fourteenth Army inflicted a comprehensive defeat on the Japanese, supported by massive aerial resupply and air superiority, which enabled transport aircraft to be used with relative safety close to the enemy. Between 18 April and 30 June some 12,550 reinforcements and 18,800 tons of supplies were delivered to Imphal and about 13,000 sick and wounded and some 43,000 noncombatants evacuated. Despite limited payloads, atrocious terrain and weather conditions, together with the effect of Japanese interdiction and limited range, transport aircraft provided Fourteenth Army in Assam, in Arakan and then in Burma with the means to continue fighting when the physical constraints of terrain prevented resupply by land.

Slim and Wingate with Brigadier-General Old (US Army Air Force) and Air Vice Marshal S. F. Vincent. Old was an American whose personal leadership saw him piloting the first supply aircraft to fly to the relief of the Admin Box at Sinzweya in Arakan in February 1944. Orde Wingate conceived and led the Chindits in 1943 and 1944. This photograph was taken on the day of the fly-in of Operation *Thursday*, March 1944. (IWM, MH 7881)

## The Burma campaign

The battles in Arakan in February, and at Imphal and Kohima decisively shattered the myth of Japanese invincibility that had for over two years crippled the Allied cause. They also set the seal on Slim's efforts to rebuild the fighting power of Fourteenth Army. The risk he had taken in allowing the Japanese to penetrate so deeply into Assam had paid off, but it had not been without its worrying moments. Slim had misjudged the speed and violence of the force that would fall on Kohima, for example, but he had kept his nerve and Fourteenth Army fought with a concentrated fury that took Mutaguchi and his army entirely by surprise. Now, with resounding success accompanying him, Slim wanted more. Despite its obvious disadvantages Slim became convinced that the only sure way of defeating the Japanese in Burma was by land, and that he would have to do it with the resources at hand. 'I believed' he wrote 'more firmly than ever, in spite of the doubts of so many, that, if we were to regain Burma, it must be by an overland advance from the north.'

But despite these victories the Chiefs of Staff in both London and Washington remained ignorant for some months not just of the scale of the Japanese defeat but also of its implications for the conduct of the war in the

Far East. Consequently, because both battle and victory had taken them by surprise, the Allies were slow to decide how to exploit the new strategic realities in the theatre. The one man who appeared alone to understand what the defeat of Fifteenth Army now meant for Japanese hegemony in Burma was Slim. He realized that he now had the opportunity not just to expel the remaining Japanese from India, but also to pursue them back into the heart of Burma. Indeed, were he to do this, he was convinced that bigger prizes were possible, perhaps even the seizure of Rangoon itself. The taste of victory in both Assam and Arakan had injected into Fourteenth Army a newfound confidence based on the irrefutable evidence that the Japanese could be beaten. 'Our troops had proved themselves in battle the superiors of the Japanese' commented Slim with satisfaction; 'they had seen them run'. By mid-1944 Slim was convinced that an aggressive policy of pursuit into Burma to exploit these victories was not just desirable but necessary.

However, few of his superiors saw Slim's vision as clearly as he did and during the remainder of 1944 Mountbatten badgered the Combined Chiefs of Staff for a decision about what to do next. On 3 June 1944 Slim had been given permission to engage in aggressive pursuit of Fifteenth Army to the Chindwin. On 2 July, however, Slim met Mountbatten and persuaded him that were Fourteenth Army to mount an offensive it could do so with no more resources than those that would anyway be allocated to the defence of India. Furthermore, he believed that an offensive could begin as early as 1 November.

Keen to engage London on the subject of the recapture of Burma, Mountbatten submitted two plans for approval on 23 July 1944. Both were planned to be conducted independently, or together. The first, Operation *Capital*, was drawn up by Slim, and was designed to take Fourteenth Army from Imphal and Stilwell's forces from Lashio deep into Burma, to a line running from the confluence of the Irrawaddy and Chindwin rivers at Pakokku through to Mandalay and then on to Lashio. The second, Operation *Dracula*, entailed an amphibious assault on Rangoon in early 1945 followed by an advance north to Mandalay to meet up with the Allied forces moving south. London's reaction to Operation *Capital* was one of hesitation. Unaware of the spectacular success of the Imphal/Kohima battle, few were willing to commit to the prospect of waging an offensive in a country which held so many bitter memories and which would self-evidently consume vast quantities of scarce resources. The Chiefs of Staff were

Slim receives his knighthood from the Viceroy of India, Field Marshal the Viscount Wavell, 16 December 1944, along with Generals Stopford, Scoones and Christison, for the destruction of the Japanese 'March on Delhi' which began with the feint in Arakan in February 1944 and ended with the complete destruction of Mutaguchi's Fifteenth Army in Manipur in August. (IWM, SE 2815)

taken by Operation *Dracula*, however, as it meant not having to wage an expensive land campaign from the north. They concluded that, while Slim's forces must on all accounts remain on the offensive, Fourteenth Army was to limit itself to holding operations until such time as Operation *Dracula* could be launched at Rangoon.

Despite this judgement, Slim was determined to press ahead with his own plans and the Chiefs of Staff's instructions to Mountbatten on 3 June 1944 gave him the opportunity he required. He was realistic enough to accept that he would never have the resources required to mount a two-corps offensive over nearly 1,000 miles (1,600km) of impossible terrain and across two of the world's largest rivers, at a time when the invasion of France loomed large in the Allies' consciousness. At the same time, however, a strategic reprioritization to allow an amphibious assault on the south-eastern seaboard of Burma on the *Dracula* model, Slim knew, was also highly unlikely.

Nevertheless, Slim believed firmly that if he didn't make the running in preparing a plan to defeat the Japanese in Burma, no one would, and a great opportunity decisively to defeat the whole of the Japanese war machine in Burma would thus be squandered. The difficulty in the aftermath of Imphal lay in bringing this vision to fruition in the face of the animosity in London and Washington to such proposals and the instructions he had already received merely to pursue Fifteenth Army to the Chindwin. Yet Slim's clear vision throughout 1944 was undoubtedly not just to destroy Mutaguchi's army, but to launch an offensive into Burma that would succeed in driving the Japanese into the sea. This vision was Slim's alone. It is difficult not to conclude that Slim succeeded in weaving his own strategic ambitions into the limited orders he received from Mountbatten and that as the months went by he allowed the momentum of successful Fourteenth Army operations to apply their own post facto legitimacy to plans that were his own rather than those of his superiors. It seems clear that his immediate superiors,

Slim with Lady Aileen Slim at Imphal after the ceremony. (IWM, SE 2716)

as well as the Chiefs of Staff, accepted Slim's successive faits accomplis not just because they worked, but because they themselves had nothing to offer as alternatives.

By September 1944 the climate had improved sufficiently for Mountbatten to secure from the Octagon Conference, meeting in Quebec, an extension of the earlier mandate. On 16 September he was given authority to capture all of Burma, provided that operations to achieve this did not prejudice the security of the air supply route to China. This was much-needed confirmation for Slim of the

direction in which he was already heading. Slim was ordered to initiate planning for Operation *Capital* to be put into effect in December.

He knew that the considerable logistical nightmare associated with relying on land-based lines of communication could in large part be overcome by the use of air supply, a factor that had played a significant part in all his operations to date. He knew also that the Japanese had received a defeat the like of which would make it difficult for them to recover quickly. 'A second great defeat for that army, properly exploited, would disrupt it and leave, not Mandalay but all Burma at our mercy' he reasoned. 'It, therefore, became my aim to force another major battle on the enemy at the earliest feasible moment.' He found himself faced with his second great chance and he was determined to seize it.

To match the new style of fighting Slim expected once the Chindwin and Irrawaddy had been crossed, Slim appointed Lieutenant-General Frank Messervy – who had commanded the 7th Indian Division in Arakan – to command a reconstructed IV Corps in October 1944. Messervy was also a bold thinker and suggested that one brigade of 17th Indian Division be mechanized and another made air transportable to exploit the new terrain Fourteenth Army would meet once the Chindwin had been breached. Slim agreed and converted 5th Indian Division to the new organization as well. Messervy's idea proved to be critical both to the success of the seizure of Meiktila in February and in the epic dash to Rangoon in April.

Slim's plan for Operation *Capital* necessitated the retraining and restructuring of his Army. Once over the Irrawaddy, the Army would have to fight in a very different style to that which had won it the great victories in Arakan, Imphal and Kohima. After two long years of jungle fighting the wide prairie-like plains of central Burma beckoned, where fast-moving armoured thrusts, large-scale artillery 'stonks' and attacks on broad fronts by brigades and divisions would replace the intense but relatively slow bayonet, rifle and grenade struggles by sections, platoons and companies in the half-gloom of the jungle that had characterized the fighting in Arakan and the hills of eastern India. Speed, the massed use of armour, bold flanking movements and the close cooperation of tanks, infantry, artillery and aircraft would define operations in this new environment after the Chindwin had been crossed. To meet this requirement Messervy's corps comprised 7th and 19th Indian Divisions and 255th Tank Brigade equipped with Sherman tanks, while XXXIII Corps (Lieutenant-General Montagu Stopford) comprised 2nd Division, 20th Indian Division, 268th Lorried Infantry Brigade

A DUKW crosses the mighty Irrawaddy in February 1945 in support of operations against Mandalay. One of the mightiest rivers in the world, Slim's two corps crossed this obstacle on a shoestring, but entirely surprised the Japanese commander, Kimura, who expected a more traditional strike from the north. Instead, Slim pretended to do what the Japanese commander expected, all the while deceiving him with a decisive strike into the Japanese's unprotected belly at Meiktila to the south of Mandalay. (IWM, SE 1556)

and 254th Tank Brigade, with Stuart and Lee-Grant tanks. During September and October 1944 considerable retraining took place in Fourteenth Army to prepare for this new style of warfighting.

Slim's determination to pursue Mutaguchi relentlessly across the Chindwin during the monsoon paid off. On 6 August 1944 – his 53rd birthday – Slim ordered Stopford, who now had responsibility for all operations east of the Manipur River, to direct his pursuit against both Kalewa and Sittaung on the Chindwin. 11th East African Division led the advance from Tamu, methodically pushing their way eastwards against last-ditch opposition. The process was slow and difficult because of continuing Japanese resistance, the appalling weather and complex terrain. Men, mules and elephants struggled down jungle tracks after the retreating Japanese, crossing swollen rivers and rebuilding collapsed tracks and roads. In the air the overstretched air forces pushed through minimal visibility to deliver their precious loads by parachute and free drop to the troops below them.

During the advance it became apparent that the scale of the Japanese defeat was far greater than expected. The detritus of Mutaguchi's fleeing army was strewn across the jungle hills, bodies and equipment littering the escape routes east. Sittaung was occupied on 4 September and by 10 September the Chindwin was crossed and a small bridgehead secured. By mid-November Kalemyo was also secured by troops from 11th East Africa Division and those of 5th Indian Division, which had pushed methodically southwards down the Tiddim road. Tiddim was then occupied on 17 October. Then Kalewa was captured by 11th East African Division on 2 December 1944. 'I had asked for the impossible' Slim remarked, 'and got it.'

During the pursuit to the Chindwin Slim had been exercised about how he could engage and defeat General Kimura Heitar – commander of the Burma Area Army – in open battle once the Chindwin had been breached. His fundamental desire was to destroy the Japanese army in Burma. Capturing territory was incidental, and would follow on naturally from the former.

A mortar crew on the advance towards Rangoon, at Toungoo in April 1945. (IWM, SE 4723)

'It was not Mandalay or Meiktila that we were after but the Japanese army,' he commented 'and that thought had to be firmly implanted in the mind of every man of the Fourteenth Army.' Slim's eyes had long been focused on the vast Shwebo Plain on the west bank of the Irrawaddy as ideal terrain for the battle he sought, a battle of manoeuvre in which his artillery, armour and air support would have a devastating effect on the Japanese and where the Japanese would would be forced to fight with their backs to the Irrawaddy.

The Shwebo Plain was 400 miles (640km) from the nearest railhead, and 250 miles (400km) were along simple earth roads impassable in the monsoon. Slim's two corps were outnumbered by Kimura's forces which, chastened but far from beaten, amounted to five and a half divisions, an independent mixed brigade, a tank regiment, nearly 40,000 line of communication troops as well as two renegade Indian National Army divisions. In northern Burma the Japanese Thirty-third Army was based on Bhamo opposing the Chinese and the reconstructed Fifteenth Army was based in central Burma defending the Irrawaddy. But Fourteenth Army's advantage in the air, in armour, in greater mobility in the open, and the spirit of his troops gave Slim the confidence to press ahead despite what otherwise would have appeared to be unacceptable odds.

Slim's assessment was that Fifteenth Army would hold a defensive line in the formidable jungle-clad mountains that lay about 25 miles (40km) to the east of the Chindwin running parallel to it for a distance of 120 miles (200km). Slim's plan was to punch through these hills with Messervy's IV Corps on the left and Stopford's XXXIII Corps on the right, both corps converging on the Ye-U–Shwebo area. IV Corps was to break out of the Sittaung bridgehead and, following an easterly course, force its way through the mountains, seize Pinlebu and thereafter change direction to capture Shwebo from the north. Stopford's XXXIII Corps, meanwhile, was tasked to advance from Kalewa on a broad front, following the general south-easterly route of the Chindwin towards Ye-U and Monywa.

In planning the offensive Slim was concerned to tell Messervy and Stopford what to do, while allowing them virtually complete freedom to decide how they carried out his instructions. Choosing one's subordinates well and then delegating responsibility to them was a strong characteristic of Slim's leadership. In Burma this approach to command made especial sense, for two reasons. First, the obvious geographical difficulties in the theatre made regular communication difficult. Second, Slim was convinced that his commanders could best achieve his requirements without him breathing down their necks while they were conducting operations. He wanted them to think and act independently, but always within the context of his overall intention. Opportunities for rapid, destabilizing attacks and armoured thrusts from unexpected quarters or at unexpected times were not to be limited by waiting for orders from above. Commanders had to be self-reliant and not dependent upon higher headquarters for direction at times when decisions needed to be made on the spot. They were expected to act quickly, boldly and decisively, to 'shoot a goal when the referee wasn't looking' as Stopford described it.

As a result of this freedom a deep mutual trust built up between Slim and his corps and divisional commanders. Major-General Geoffrey Evans, who as GOC of first 5th and then 7th Indian Division, had direct experience of Slim's style of command and believed that this approach allowed commanders 'to adapt their tactics according to the country... and to make the most of what was given to them; encouraged to use their initiative, they

# Slim's reconquest of Burma

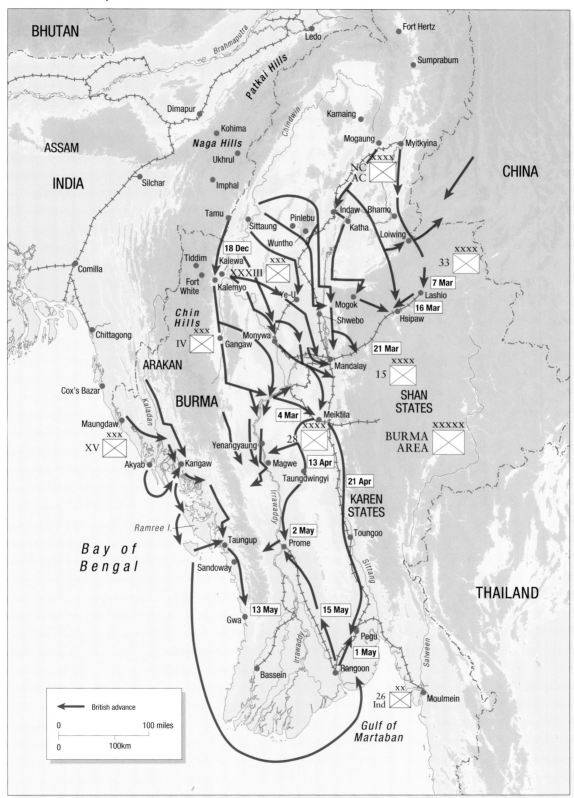

BHUTAN

Brahmaputra

Ledo

Fort Hertz

Sumprabum

Patkai Hills

Dimapur

Chindwin

Kamaing

Kohima

*Naga Hills*

Mogaung

Myitkyina

CHINA

ASSAM

Ukhrul

NC
AC

XXXX

INDIA

Silchar

Imphal

Tamu

Sittaung

Pinlebu

Indaw

Bhamo

Wuntho

Katha

Tiddim

**18 Dec**

Kalewa

Loiwing

XXXIII

XXX

33

XXXX

Comilla

Fort
White

Kalemyo

Ye-U

**7 Mar**

Mogok

Lashio

*Chin
Hills*

Shwebo

**16 Mar**

Chittagong

IV

XXX

Monywa

Hsipaw

Gangaw

**21 Mar**

ARAKAN

Mandalay

15

XXXX

Cox's Bazar

*Kaladan*

BURMA

SHAN
STATES

Maungdaw

Meiktila

**4 Mar**

XV

XXX

BURMA
AREA

XXXXX

Akyab

Kangaw

Yenangyaung

28

XXXX

Magwe

**13 Apr**

Taungdwingyi

*Irrawaddy*

**21 Apr**

*Ramree I.*

KAREN
STATES

*Bay of
Bengal*

Taungup

Toungoo

Sandoway

**2 May**

Prome

*Sittang*

THAILAND

**13 May**

**15 May**

Gwa

*Irrawaddy*

Pegu

*Salween*

**1 May**

Bassein

Rangoon

0              100 miles
⟵ British advance

0         100km

26
Ind

XX

Moulmein

*Gulf of
Martaban*

Royal Welsh Fusiliers on patrol near the Chindwin, November 1944. (IWM, SE 2889)

did so without fear. And such was Slim's confidence in them that once plans were made and orders issued, he left them to fight the battle in their own way, making himself and his staff always available to help.'

Wasting no time Fourteenth Army crossed the Chindwin as soon as it was reached. Slim urged Messervy to advance as quickly as possible and to take risks that would months before have been unthinkable, in order to maintain the momentum of the advance. The vanguard of his corps was led by 19th Indian Division. Advancing across the Chindwin at Sittaung on 4 December 1944, it headed rapidly east, and less than two weeks later had joined up with forces driving south from northern Burma, part of General Sultan's successful drive south from Lashio against Thirty-third Army. Surprisingly, Japanese resistance was far less intense than had been expected. Nevertheless, the advance was an extraordinary effort given the appalling nature of the terrain. Roads had to be hacked out of the virgin jungle by troops using what tools they could carry.

Further south a brigade of the 20th Indian Division led the XXXIII Corps advance, crossing the Chindwin north of Kalewa, while 11th East African Division fought hard to extend the Kalewa bridgehead. By 10 December, in an extraordinary logistical and engineering achievement, the largest Bailey bridge then in existence – 1,154ft (350m) long – had been thrown across the river. On 18 December the remainder of 20th Indian Division followed through the bridgehead.

Within days of the start of IV Corps' advance, however, Slim accepted that his initial plan to trap Kimura on the Shwebo Plain in front of the Irrawaddy would not work. The weakness of the opposition facing 19th Indian Division forced him to recognize that Kimura had withdrawn the bulk of his forces east of the Irrawaddy, with the obvious intention of fighting behind, rather than in front of, the river, and mauling Fourteenth Army as it attempted to cross. If this were to happen Fourteenth Army would be stretched out from Tamu and vulnerable to counterattack just when it was attempting to cross one of the most formidable river barriers in the world.

Slim refused to countenance such folly. He sought, instead, a means not only of crossing his five divisions and three tank brigades without mishap or significant interference over the Irrawaddy but also of creating the decisive advantage he required to bring the Japanese to battle on his own terms. He wanted to fight Kimura where he, Slim, was strongest and where Kimura was weakest. He needed something more cunning and subtle than the simple though casualty-laden battering-ram approach.

To achieve this goal Slim's eyes turned to the towns of Meiktila and Thazi, lying approximately 70 miles (113km) south of Mandalay. These towns were the key nodal points on Kimura's supply infrastructure, supporting all of his army. The railway and main road from Rangoon ran through Meiktila before bending north towards Mandalay, and the town formed a natural location for supply and ammunition dumps, airfields and hospitals. If Slim could cut off the Japanese from this vital logistical centre, their ability to resist Stopford's inexorable pressure in the

An infantry patrol near Kohima, on the alert for snipers, June 1944. (IWM, SE 3479)

north around Mandalay would be fatally weakened. Slim recognized that, without Meiktila, Kimura could not hope to sustain a prolonged battle for Mandalay. Indeed, it might even prove to be the decisive act in the destruction of the whole of Kimura's army.

Within days Slim and his staff had come up with a plan, which he dubbed Operation *Extended Capital*. The idea was to make Kimura believe that nothing had changed, and that Slim would attempt to cross both XXXIII and IV Corps over the Irrawaddy north-west of Mandalay. Slim's revised plan, however, was that while XXXIII Corps would continue to cross the Irrawaddy to the north of Mandalay, as originally planned, IV Corps (reconfigured for the operation to comprise 7th and 17th Indian Divisions, 28th East African Brigade and 255th Tank Brigade) would instead cross the river in great secrecy far to the south before striking hard with armour, motorized artillery and infantry at Meiktila.

The northern advance by XXXIII Corps (strengthened by 19th Indian Division and 268th Brigade) would be a deception to hide the decisive strike by IV Corps to the south. If Slim could attract the greatest possible number of enemy divisions towards the northern crossing points he could minimize opposition to the real focus of his attack in the south. This would provide Slim with, as he put it, 'not only the major battle I desired, but the chance to repeat our old hammer and anvil tactics: XXXIII Corps the hammer from the north against the anvil of IV Corps at Meiktila – and the Japanese between.' Had the aircraft been available, Slim would have employed airborne forces to capture Meiktila, but in the circumstances this was not possible.

Slim explained his revised plan to Messervy and Stopford on 18 December, and on 19 December issued his plan. Confident in their commander, both men quickly translated it into action. Indeed, the XXXIII Corps advance continued unabated during this period. The leading troops of 2nd Division, together with the Lee-Grant and Stuart tanks of 254th Tank Brigade, passed through Pyingaing (known to the troops as 'Pink

Gin') on 23 December. Japanese rearguards attempted to hold up the advance through ambushes and mining but to no avail, and the important airfield at Ye-U was captured on 2 January 1945. Three days later the division had established a firm bridgehead over the Mu River, and both it and 19th Indian Division now began a race for Shwebo, with the Japanese 15th Division streaming before it in full retreat to the Irrawaddy. Shwebo was captured on 9 January jointly by units of both divisions. The 19th Indian Division had reached the Shwebo area by 5 January, established bridgeheads over the Irrawaddy and began to advance southwards on the east bank of the river towards Mandalay.

Slim's plan was bold. Surprise and secrecy were essential. But it also depended entirely on his ability to supply his armoured spearheads as they penetrated deep into Japanese-held territory. Some idea of the distances that had to be covered can be envisaged when one considers that the distance between Imphal and Rangoon represents a comparable distance between London and Marseilles: Burma's 240,000 square miles (620,000 square kilometres) could easily fill both France and Belgium. The administrative effort to supply two corps well forward of their supply bases in inhospitable terrain was formidable. XXXIII Corps had to push rapidly forwards in the north while IV Corps, with its armour, moved in secret down 330 miles (530km) of rough dirt track from Tamu to the area of Pakokku before conducting an opposed crossing of one of the world's mightiest rivers.

The physical restraint of operating in difficult terrain long distances from railheads meant that Slim was able to sustain over the Chindwin no more than four and two-thirds divisions and two tank brigades. However, the decisive advantage the Allies enjoyed in the air meant that he could rely on air transport to maintain his forward units, so long as the requisite numbers of aircraft remained available. With the vast experience of Arakan, of Operation *Thursday* and of the airlift into Imphal and Kohima in 1944, the air supply organization supporting Fourteenth Army had become the model of its kind.

RAF aircrews preparing bombs at a forward base in Burma, February 1945. (IWM, CF 355).

Having sufficient aircraft was a constant problem. Slim's plans were dealt a devastating blow on the morning of 10 December 1944 when he awoke at Imphal to the sound of mass aircraft activity at the nearby airfield. Slim quickly discovered that 75 of his precious USAAF Dakota transport aircraft were being diverted to meet a developing crisis in China. Slim immediately told Mountbatten that without these aircraft the success of Operation *Capital* could not be guaranteed. Mountbatten fought hard to have the aircraft returned, and on 21 January two of the three squadrons Slim had lost were returned to him. Aircraft range, however, soon became an issue of strategic importance. Once the Chindwin had been crossed, the forward supply bases in eastern India, which had played a crucial role in the survival of the Imphal pocket, became too far distant for supply aircraft to fly economically. Consequently the capture of airfields along the route of Slim's advance was essential to provide the very minimum of support his forces required to sustain offensive operations. The initial objectives for *Capital*, therefore, were the Burmese airfields west of the Chindwin.

Japanese dead at Meiktila, March 1945. Kimura fought desperately to unlock the hold that Slim held on his vitals in this key nodal point supporting the Japanese defence of the Irrawaddy shore. He failed, and his troops suffered enormous loss of life. (IWM, IND 4592)

The closest possible form of cooperation between Fourteenth Army, the RAF and the USAAF was built up in 1944, and the benefits were reaped in abundance during the campaign of 1945. When Slim moved his headquarters to Imphal in October 1944 he colocated it with the Headquarters of the RAF's 221 Group. Henceforth both headquarters 'lived side by side, worked and moved as one' to become an effective joint headquarters. Throughout Operation *Extended Capital* the Allied air forces flew some 7,000 sorties a day to sustain and support the land offensive. By April 1945 nearly 90 per cent of Fourteenth Army's supplies were provided by air. From January through to the third week in May 1945 the army received some 5,500 tons by road, 38,600 tons by river, and 210,000 tons by air. 'To us,' wrote Slim, 'all this was as normal as moving or maintaining troops by railway or road.'

Indeed, Slim regarded Operation *Extended Capital* not to be a Fourteenth Army offensive at all, but a joint air-land campaign in which land and air elements were equal partners. Slim could rightly claim that operations by Fourteenth Army throughout 1944 and 1945 provided a distinctive contribution 'towards a new kind of warfare.' Slim's judgement was unequivocal. 'Throughout the entire campaign 14th Army had proved right in our reliance on the air forces…' he wrote, 'first to gain control of the air, and then to supply, transport and support us. The campaign had been an air one, as well as a land one. Without the victory of the air forces there would have been no victory for the army.'

But while air transport answered some of Slim's most pressing needs, theland-based line of communication that stretched some 500 miles (800km) back to Dimapur also required substantial work to ensure that Fourteenth Army could operate far ahead of its bases. Road building and upgrading was essential, but the resources to achieve this feat – aircraft,

Tanks and infantry cooperate closely together during the advance to Rangoon, May 1945. (IWM, IND 4650)

Japanese troops surrender in 1945, the empire they had built on blood in 1941 and 1942 proved to be a short-lived, expensive folly. (IWM, IND 4858)

motor transport, and engineer equipment – were extremely limited. Slim had therefore to turn the received wisdom regarding logistics on its head. At the beginning of the war Slim had been advised never to commit himself to operations without the necessary resources to see it through. For 100 years the British Army, Slim observed, unlike the Japanese, 'had tended to stress supply at the expense of mobility'.

This constant crisis of resources, however, had a positive effect on the men of Fourteenth Army, forcing them to become self-reliant and innovative. Self-help, ingenuity and improvisation became special virtues. Railways were extended, roads built and surfaced, sunken ferries refloated and repaired. Slim's chief engineer, Bill Hasted, invented a means of hardening road surfaces by laying on them strips of hessian soaked in tar, called 'bithess'. 'For over a hundred miles this novel surface proved able to take a thousand vehicles a day when the monsoon came.' Hasted, likewise, felled forests to make barges able to carry 10 tons each, in order to make best use of the Chindwin as a supply artery. Three of these tied together could carry a Sherman tank. Outboard engines were flown in, boat wrecks were repaired and even sunken vessels on the riverbed were recovered, repaired and pressed into service. These and other measures were so successful that whereas in November 1943 an average of 2,800 tons a day were moved forwards, by September 1944 this had increased to 6,500 tons and by March 1945 nearly 9,000 tons a day.

The march south by IV Corps began on 19 January and, despite the difficulties of the terrain, moved quickly. Slim had given Messervy 15 February as the last acceptable date for crossing the Irrawaddy. Elaborate deception measures were adopted to ensure that his move through the jungle to Pakokku remained concealed from the Japanese, and to reinforce in Kimura's mind the certain belief that IV Corps remained with XXXIII Corps on the Shwebo Plain. While the real IV Corps had to keep radio silence during its move southwards a dummy corps headquarters was established in Tamu, using the same radio frequencies, through which

all communications from 19th Indian Division to XXXIII Corps had to pass. Despite the inconvenience this caused for commanders, this complicated deception was spectacularly successful.

The Japanese did not believe that a large-scale advance through the Gangaw Valley was possible. Unobserved and unhindered Messervy's forward units were only 40 miles (60km) from the Irrawaddy by late January. Kimura, while aware of some activity on his southern flank, regarded this to be nothing more than demonstrations by minor forces designed to draw him south, and he was not to be tempted into doing something so foolish. All the while he continued to reinforce the Irrawaddy in the Mandalay area, bringing in all available forces from across Burma, so that by February he had a force equivalent to eight Japanese and one and a third Indian National Army divisions. He was confident that these would be more than sufficient to defeat the expected five divisions of Fourteenth Army in what he was now calling the decisive 'Battle of the Irrawaddy Shore'. His failure to appreciate the overall subtlety of Slim's approach, the dynamism and mobility of Fourteenth Army, together with the extraordinary power and flexibility afforded to Slim by virtue of air transport and air superiority, proved to be the major strands in his undoing.

The advantage was now Slim's: only six weeks after he had changed his plan Fourteenth Army was before the Irrawaddy on a 200-mile (320km) front with IV Corps about to cross the river in the area of Pakokku. The advance of Fourteenth Army had been so rapid that Mountbatten reported to London on 23 February 1945 that Operation *Dracula* was no longer required as Slim appeared likely to seize Rangoon before the onset of the monsoon in May. With XXXIII Corps placing growing pressure on the Japanese in the region of Mandalay, the timing of the main crossings became increasingly crucial – too soon and Kimura would recognize the threat to his southern flank and deploy his reserves to counter it; too late and the pressure on XXXIII Corps might be sufficient to halt its advance on Mandalay.

British tanks prepare to assault Meiktila, February 1945. The dramatic impact made by armour during the 1944 and 1945 campaigns made laughable the claims made by some in New Delhi in 1943 that armour could not operate in Burma. Slim had seen the magnificent work done by the 7th Armoured Brigade during the retreat in 1942, and insisted on deploying them forwards into the battle areas in Arakan and Manipur. The thrust against Meiktila in February 1944 was a highly successful all-arms force of armour, infantry, artillery and integrated air power. (IWM, SE 3276)

In early February Stopford made successive and determined efforts from the north to capture Mandalay, reinforcing the impression that this was Slim's point of main effort. Nearly three Japanese divisions made attacks against the 19th Indian Division bridgehead and Kimura, believing that this was the likely location of Fourteenth Army's principal attack, provided additional artillery and some of his remaining tanks to this area. However, it was to no avail; as the bridgehead strengthened, the Japanese were

slowly pushed back. Meanwhile 20th Indian Division approached Monywa and took the town after hard fighting in mid-January, and on 8 February Slim moved his headquarters to the town that he had vacated during the retreat in May 1942. Other troops from 20th Indian Division arrived alongside the Irrawaddy west of Mandalay and began to cross on the night of 12 February. The Japanese were slow to oppose this incursion but when they did it was with desperate fury, waves of attacks taking place during the ensuing fortnight against the two bridgeheads, many during daylight.

The real focus of Slim's offensive, of course, lay far to the south. The first crossings by 7th Indian Division began at the tiny fishing village of Nyaungu on the night of 13 February although it took four days to establish a bridgehead, 6,000 yards wide by 4,000 yards deep (5,500 by 3,650m). Messervy's plan was that 17th Indian Division, together with the Sherman tanks of 255th Tank Brigade, would then pass rapidly across the river to seize Meiktila. Elaborate deception measures were adopted to cover the Nyaungu crossings. 28th East African Brigade pretended to parry south to recover the Chauk and Yenangyaung oilfields, dummy parachute drops were made east of Chauk to reinforce this picture and 17th Indian Division applied heavy pressure on Pakokku to make out that crossings were also intended there. These deception schemes were undoubtedly successful and acted to hide from Japanese comprehension, until it was too late, the reality of Slim's strategy. A captured Japanese intelligence officer later explained that they did not believe that there was more than one division in the area, and that it was directed down the west bank towards Yenangyaung.

British infantry search village huts on the outskirts of Meiktila, March 1945 as part of the operations against Kimura's southern dispositions on the Irrawaddy. (IWM, SE 3102)

This was a period of acute anxiety for Slim. The administrative risks he had taken now looked alarmingly great. All but one of his divisions (5th Indian Division) was engaged; as the tempo increased so too did Fourteenth Army's expenditure of petrol and ammunition, increasing the strain on the already stretched line of communication. The strain was apparent only to those who knew him best. It was the only time his RAF commander, with whom he shared his headquarters, ever saw Slim tense. He 'was a little quieter than usual' he recalled, 'and one was conscious that there was a bit of worry going on'.

His problems were compounded by the fact that on 23 February Chiang Kai-shek suddenly demanded the redeployment to China of all American and Chinese forces in the Northern Combat Area Command, and that American transport squadrons should fly them out. If Kimura withdrew the forces that he had facing the NCAC and threw them into the battle about Mandalay instead, at a time when he faced the loss of more of his precious aircraft, Fourteenth Army operations would undoubtedly have

halted completely. But the threat was lifted in part by the US Chiefs of Staff agreeing after representation from Mountbatten and the British Chiefs of Staff to leave the bulk of their transport squadrons in Burma until the capture of Rangoon or 1 June 1945, whichever was the earlier.

Meanwhile, the decisive struggle for Meiktila was taking place. Cowan advanced out of Nyaungu on 21 February. The Japanese commander of the Meiktila area had some 12,000 troops as well as 1,500 miscellaneous base troops and hospital patients at his disposal for the defence of the town, and every man able to carry a weapon, fit or otherwise, was pressed into service. Messervy's aim was to seize the town as quickly as possible, with the road to be cleared subsequently by 7th Indian Division once the security of the Irrawaddy bridgehead was firm. Cowan's plan was to use his armour to punch through the Japanese lines to seize an airfield 12 miles (19km) east of Meiktila, to allow for the fly-in of a brigade, while neighbouring villages were either captured or screened by his other two brigades. The whole division with the armour would then assault Meiktila.

While 63rd Brigade brushed aside light opposition to move up closer to the town's western defences, 48th Brigade began moving north-east as 255th Tank Brigade, with two infantry battalions and a self-propelled 25-pdr battery under command, moved to a position east of Meiktila. The armour, deployed in wide flanking aggressive actions, caught the Japanese defenders in the open and inflicted heavy casualties on them. With the jungle now behind them, 17th Indian Division's tanks, mechanized artillery and mechanized infantry found the flat lands beyond the Irrawaddy well suited to the tactics of encircling and cutting off Japanese positions.

The Japanese had no answer to either Fourteenth Army's use of armour or to the effectiveness of the all-arms tactics in which it was employed. When Meiktila was reached, an immediate attack was put in, with all available artillery and air support. The attack penetrated well, but resistance was fierce and fanatical. Yet again, the Japanese soldier showed his penchant for fighting to the death. During 2 and 3 March, two infantry brigades, together with the Sherman tanks of 255th Tank Brigade, closed in from differing points of the compass, squeezing and destroying the Japanese between them. By 6pm on 3 March Meiktila fell. During 4 and 5 March even the most fanatical points of resistance were brushed aside as surrounding villages were cleared and the main airfield secured.

Kimura was shocked, as Slim knew he would be, by the sudden and unexpected loss of Meiktila. He at once sought to crush 17th Indian Division and recapture the town, and for three weeks from mid-March the Japanese

Air Vice Marshal S. F. Vincent, Air Officer Commander of No. 221 Group RAF (centre), watches Hawker Hurricanes take off from Sadaung, Burma, on a strafing operation during the advance on Mandalay, with Slim (right), and Group Captain D. O. Finlay, Commanding Officer of No. 906 Wing RAF (left). (IWM, CF 325)

mounted a series of ferocious counterattacks against 17th Indian Division. Once in Meiktila the British policy was one of 'aggressive defence'. Combined arms groups of infantry, mechanized artillery and armour, supported from the air by attack aircraft, were sent out every day to hunt, ambush and destroy approaching Japanese columns in a radius of 20 miles (32km) from the town. The pressure on Meiktila built up, however. Soon the land line of communication back to Nyaungu was cut, and the Japanese tried hard to seize the airfield.

The situation was sufficiently disconcerting for Slim to decide to commit his last remaining reserve, 5th Indian Division, which arrived onto one of the Meiktila airfields, under enemy fire, on 17 March. This was a huge risk for Slim. But he knew that if he did not secure victory in this battle he would have to concede the campaign. His gamble paid off. By 29 March the Japanese were beaten back, losing their guns and suffering heavy casualties in the process. The river port of Myingyan on the Chindwin was captured after a fierce fight, and its rapid commissioning as a working port substantially reduced the pressure on Messervy's land line of communication. Before long it was receiving 200 tons of desperately needed supplies every day.

Slim's relief at the securing of the Meiktila battlefield was palpable, and he gave thanks where it was due. He was in no doubt that the success first in seizing Meiktila, then in holding the town against increasingly frantic Japanese counterattacks, secured the success of Operation *Extended Capital*. The battle was, he reflected, 'a magnificent feat of arms… [which] sealed the fate of the Japanese in Burma'. This was no overstatement. IV Corps' thrust against Meiktila was Slim's decisive stroke, on which the success of his entire strategy rested, and for which he had subordinated everything else. Now, the huge risks he had taken had come good. The Japanese also were in no doubt about the significance of Slim's victory, Kimura admitting in captivity that it was 'the masterpiece of Allied strategy' in the battle for Burma. The historian Louis Allen regarded it to be 'Slim's greatest triumph', a feat that allowed him to place 'his hand firmly on the jugular of the Japanese' and which put 'the final reconquest of Burma within Slim's grasp'.

Slim now needed to attack Kimura hard in order to prevent him from turning against the IV Corps anvil forming around Meiktila. When this anvil was firm Slim intended to allow XXXIII Corps – the hammer – to fall on Kimura hard from the north. The first part of this hammer – 19th Indian Division – broke out of its bridgehead 40 miles (64km) north of Mandalay on 26 February.

Slim entering Mandalay with Pete Rees driving, March 1945, being cheered by his men. This sort of scene is memorable for its rarity. Few British commanders – Marlborough, Wellington, Nelson among a very few – experienced the public adulation of his soldiers as Bill Slim did. (IWM, SE 3530)

By 4 March the division was in tankable country 20 miles (32km) north of Mandalay, reaching the northern outskirts three days later. The two strongpoints – Mandalay Hill and Fort Dufferin – were vigorously defended and required considerable effort to overcome, but were captured by 20 March. While Mandalay was being vested, one brigade struck secretly eastward at Maymyo where they fell upon the town, taking the garrison completely by surprise.

The second part of the XXXIII Corps advance – the 20th Indian and 2nd Divisions – broke out of their respective bridgeheads to the west of Mandalay in early March. The Japanese were everywhere pushed back, losing heavily in men and artillery. Slim deduced that Kimura would attempt to hold a line running south-west from Kyaukse to Chauk, with Fifteenth Army holding the right, Thirty-third Army the centre, and Twenty-eighth Army the left. He knew that despite Japanese efforts to stiffen the line it would still be weak. Accordingly he aimed to concentrate at weak points in the line, and strike decisively at the Japanese command and communication network to remove the last vestiges of control Japanese commanders had over the course of the battle.

Closely supported by the RAF, 20th Indian Division led the charge. Two brigades sliced through the Japanese opposition to converge on Kyaukse, while another carried out a wide encircling movement to seize Wundwin, on the main railway 60 miles (96km) south of Mandalay on 21 March, although stubborn resistance prevented Kyaukse from falling until the end of the month. Throughout this period his planning cycle remained well ahead of Kimura's. 'No sooner was a plan made to meet a given situation than, due to a fresh move by Slim, it was out-of-date before it could be executed, and a new one had to be hurriedly prepared with a conglomeration of widely scattered units and formations' wrote Geoffrey Evans, watching this at first hand. 'Because of the kaleidoscopic changes in the situation, breakdowns in communication and the fact that Burma Area Army Headquarters was often out of touch with reality, many of the attacks to restore the position were uncoordinated.' The Japanese now retreated in disarray, breaking into little groups of fugitives seeking refuge in the Shan Hills to the east.

Slim's prize – Rangoon – now lay before him. Leaving the remnants of Kimura's army to fall back to the west and south-west Slim drove his army relentlessly on throughout April in a desperate race to reach the coast before the monsoon rains made the roads impassable. In a brilliantly paced campaign against the rapidly disintegrating – but still fanatical –

Slim, Mountbatten and Leese. Mountbatten understood only too well that he owed his victories in India in 1944 and Burma in 1945 to Bill Slim. His equivocation over Leese's attempt to remove Slim in 1945 is therefore all the harder to understand. Leese failed in his attempt, and Slim was appointed commander, Allied Land Forces South East Asia (ALFSEA) in his place. Leese returned to the UK in disgrace. (IWM, IND 4691)

On the Embankment during a visit to London, June 1945. Looking thin and tired, he had just been through the saga of his attempted sacking by Leese. He and Aileen were in Britain for the first time since the war began. He knew at this stage that he was to retain command of Fourteenth Army; what he did not know was that the decision to elevate him to the command of the whole of ALFSEA was about to be made by Alanbrooke, the CIGS. (IWM, D 25026)

Japanese army, Rangoon was captured only a week after the first rains fell. Messervy's corps had the lead. Punching forwards as fast as their fuel would allow, isolating and bypassing significant opposition, his armour raced from airstrip to airstrip, where engineers prepared for the fly-in of aircraft under the noses of the enemy. Fearing that the Japanese might have garrisoned Rangoon to defend it to the last, Slim had earlier persuaded Mountbatten to revive Operation *Dracula* and launch an attack from the sea to coincide with the armoured onrush from the north. In fact, the retreating Japanese had evacuated Rangoon and 26th Indian Division, landing from the sea, captured the city without a fight.

In May 1945 the war was far from over. Three more months of hard fighting were to follow as the troops of Fourteenth Army drove back the tenacious Japanese rearguards over the Karen Hills and Sittang River towards Thailand. Nevertheless the capture of Rangoon set the seal on a brilliantly fought campaign that brought about the defeat of the Japanese in Burma. It was a campaign that the strategists had never planned in the first place and its overwhelming success, like that at Imphal/Kohima the year before, came as something of a surprise to those both in London and Washington who continued to underestimate both Fourteenth Army and its commander. Slim's unhesitating switch of plan to Operation *Extended Capital* in mid-December 1944, his acceptance of the administrative and tactical risks that this entailed and his command of every nuance of the 1945 offensive as it unfolded showed him to be the consummate master of war.

Not everyone was happy, however, for Slim to receive the accolades for his remarkable achievement. As Rangoon fell Slim was informed by General Oliver Leese, the new commander of Allied Land Forces South East Asia (ALFSEA) that Slim would not command his Fourteenth Army in the forthcoming invasion planned for Malaya, instead taking command of the new Twelfth Army being formed to mop up in Burma. It was an extraordinary decision, which refused to acknowledge the spectacular success Slim had achieved. Slim saw it as a sacking, as did his men, when news spread across the Fourteenth Army. General Brooke, the Chief of the Imperial General Staff and General Auchinleck, the C-in-C India were both furious at not being consulted and brought pressure to bear on Mountbatten to in turn sack Leese. This was done, Leese returning to the UK and a premature retirement. On 1 July 1945, Slim was promoted to general and was informed that he was to succeed Leese as C-in-C ALFSEA.

It was while returning to the Far East to take up his new appointment alongside Mountbatten in Kandy in August that Slim heard the news that the atom bomb had been dropped on Japan, heralding the end of the war. On 12 September he sat in Singapore with Mountbatten to receive the unconditional surrender of all Japanese forces in South-east Asia. Disobeying

General MacArthur's stricture that Japanese officers were not to be forced to surrender their swords, Slim insisted that in South-east Asia all Japanese officers were to surrender their swords to British officers of similar or higher rank. 'Field-Marshal Terauchi's sword is in Admiral Mountbatten's hands' Slim later wrote; 'General Kimura's is now on my mantelpiece, where I always intended that one day it should be.'

Admiral Lord Louis Mountbatten gives a public address from the steps of the Municipal Buildings in Singapore during the surrender ceremony on 12 September 1945. To the left of Mountbatten are Admiral Power and Slim (now C-in-C ALFSEA) and to the right Lieutenant-General Wheeler and Air Chief Marshal Sir Keith Park. (IWM, CF 720)

# OPPOSING COMMANDERS

Slim's principal enemy in India in 1944 was Lieutenant-General Mutaguchi Renya, commander of Fifteenth Army. In Burma in 1945 he was opposed by Lieutenant-General Kimura Heitar  commander of the Burma Area Army. Mutaguchi was 55 in 1944 and Kimura, in 1945, was 56.

Mutaguchi Renya was a larger-than-life character, a man with an irrepressible, optimistic and excitable personality. He was a committed militarist. As a regimental commander in China in 1937 he had played a significant role bringing about the expansion of the war and as commander of 18th Division received the glory of capturing Singapore. From his earliest days as a soldier, Mutaguchi's personal bravery, courage and contempt for death had created an uneasy relationship with those whom he commanded. They did not love him, but his dynamism and aggressive leadership nevertheless generated considerable respect. He was a glory-hunter, and the lives of his men were incidental to his achievement of military fame. Unfortunately, his men knew this. They knew him to be a plain-speaking and somewhat self-serving soldier, eager for battlefield glory and always in the thick of the fighting – but also a man for whom the welfare of his soldiers was not his first consideration.

His single greatest personal failing was his inability to engender loyalty amongst his subordinate commanders. His bombast and bullying created enemies amongst men whom he urgently needed on his side, and created a climate of fear in his own headquarters, where officers, worried about the abuse they would receive, were fearful of giving him unpalatable information.

During 1943 Mutaguchi became a passionate advocate of plans to invade India. At the time, this idea had few supporters in the Japanese Army, but it was a significant demonstration of his persuasiveness and single-mindedness that the plans were eventually accepted. The strategic rationale for Operation *C* was not to launch an 'invasion' of India but merely to extend the Japanese outer defensive perimeter across the Chindwin and into Manipur and the Naga Hills, the centre of which was Imphal, the home of Lieutenant-General

Mutaguchi as a POW. The bombastic architect of Operation *C* humbled in front of his troops as a prisoner of war. With the complete collapse of the offensive, Mutaguchi was himself relieved of command and recalled to Tokyo. He was forced into retirement in December 1944. At the end of the war he was extradited to Singapore, where he was convicted of war crimes relating to the capture of Singapore in 1942. Released from prison in March 1948, he returned to Japan and died in Tokyo in August 1966. (Popperfoto, 79621650)

Geoffrey Scoones' IV Indian Corps, which constituted the main land threat to Japanese control in Burma.

Mutaguchi knew, from what he had seen in Malaya and Singapore, that taking risks against the British always brought with it great rewards. The capture of British supply dumps formed a key assumption in his planning, confidently assuming that the three Japanese and one Indian National Army division allocated for Operation *C* would take three weeks to fall on the British supply dumps. Accordingly, he ordered that his men be equipped with rations for only 20 days. Without the capture of these supplies success could not be guaranteed, but it seemed inconceivable to Mutaguchi that a decisive and overwhelming attack against Imphal would not bring with it rapid and substantial rewards. At no time was he concerned that he might not secure these supplies.

Mutaguchi's plan was daring, inventive and aggressive. He intended to seize Imphal by a combination of guile and extreme physical endurance, seeking to achieve the same advantages that the tactic of 'swift onslaught' had brought successive Japanese commanders in their encounters with the British Army in the past. The trap he laid for Generals Slim and Scoones was to make them believe that the main attack was to be placed against Imphal, whereas in fact Mutaguchi's strategic eye lay on Kohima as a route through to Dimapur. Part of the 33rd Division in the south and south-east would advance against Major-General 'Punch' Cowan's experienced 17th Indian Division at Tiddim, destroy it and then drive due north into the unprotected underbelly of the Imphal Plain. Simultaneously, the 15th Division would attack from the east along the Tamu road, whilst the whole of 31st Division – nearly 20,000 men – would make for Kohima.

Perhaps the most debilitating aspect of Mutaguchi's planning was the conspicuous lack of enthusiasm by his original divisional commanders for the offensive. Mutaguchi failed to persuade them of its virtues, and thereafter, by the power of his own personal leadership, to bind their commitment to his. Mutaguchi in fact enjoyed extremely poor relations with each of his three divisional commanders, and because of this failed to convince them of the merits of his plan. Sato (of 31st Division) and Mutaguchi loathed each other. Yamauchi (of 15th Division) regarded the Army commander to be a 'blockhead' and 'unfit to be in command of an army'. Yanagida (of 33rd Division) likewise had a poor opinion of his Army commander, considering him to be a womanizing bore and a bully. The loathing was reciprocated. Mutaguchi had little time for either Yamauchi or Yanagida. These mutual animosities at the heart of the operation, well known to all at Headquarters Burma Area Army (Rangoon) and Headquarters South Army (Saigon), doomed Operation *C* from the start. It was Mutaguchi's poor relationship with Sato, however, who commanded the thrust against

Kohima, that had the greatest strategic impact of all on his plans for a successful offensive. The precise letter of Mutaguchi's instructions ordered him to attack Imphal, and made no mention of Dimapur. But Mutaguchi had in mind something more dramatic for the 31st Division than merely providing a guard on the new defence line at Kohima or blocking the road to Imphal. Rather, his ambition was that Sato, after capturing Kohima and refuelling his division from captured British supplies found there, would strike out to sever the head of the weakly defended Dimapur supply base from the remainder of Slim's Fourteenth Army, a move that would unlock the Brahmaputra Valley and the whole of Bengal to the invading Japanese. It would also cut the line of communication to Stilwell's Chinese forces at Ledo. In Mutaguchi's view Kohima was but a staging post on the route to Imphal and held no other strategic value: Dimapur was the jewel in the British strategic crown. If it were lost it would deal a catastrophic blow to the British, and would inevitably lead to the collapse of Imphal. Defeat would badly damage British morale, as well as removing the best place from where the Allies could mount a counter-offensive by land into Burma.

Clearly, the key to achieving this was to persuade Sato of his plan. Unfortunately, Mutaguchi did not even try. Sato was aware of what Mutaguchi wanted to do, but remained unconvinced of the strategic virtues of his plan, and therefore unwilling to commit himself wholeheartedly to its achievement. Mutaguchi's fervent commitment to the principles of bushido led him to assume that all that Sato would need was the requisite order to head for Dimapur, and that Sato would immediately and unthinkingly obey. It was a foolish assumption, and led him to ignore the need to spend time with Sato to explain what he wanted to achieve, and why, and the logistical assumptions upon which his plan was based. Because of Mutaguchi's inability to communicate effectively with his own divisional commanders, Sato remained outside of Mutaguchi's thinking from the start.

In Mutaguchi's eagerness to launch an offensive he also failed to appreciate the nature of the changes that had taken place in British warfighting capabilities during the period, and indeed of his own weaknesses. When he launched his offensive in early March 1944 the British fought hard, but also began to withdraw, which confirmed Mutaguchi in his thinking about the 'weak' British. Jubilant, he pressed his divisional commanders hard. Unfortunately for them, they found that they could not break through anywhere. They fought desperately hard, but neither at Tiddim, south of Imphal, on the Shenam heights to the south-east, in the Naga Hills to the east nor north (at Kohima) could the Japanese prevail. By virtue of tough fighting the British, supported by artillery, tanks and 300 relief planes each day, utterly destroyed Mutaguchi's offensive.

The starving and battered remnants of the once-proud Japanese army that had begun its much-vaunted 'March on Delhi' four months before began, in early June, to limp slowly and painfully away from Kohima and the hills skirting the eastern edge of the Imphal Plain. It had been decisively and comprehensively beaten, and the exhausted survivors faced the daunting prospect of a long and painful withdrawal across 100 miles (160km) of jungle-clad mountains to the relative safety of the Chindwin, all the while fleeing from the aggressive pursuit of Slim's victorious army. Fifteenth Army's command structure disintegrated. Of the 65,000 fighting troops who set off across the Chindwin in early March 1944, 30,000 were killed in battle and a further 23,000 were wounded. Only 600 allowed themselves to be taken prisoner, most of them too sick even to take their own lives. Some 17,000 pack animals perished during the operation and not a single piece of heavy weaponry made it back to Burma.

The result of Operation *C* was to create the conditions that allowed Slim's Fourteenth Army to cross the Chindwin into Burma later in 1944, sucked into the vacuum created by the retreating, devastated, Fifteenth Army. Here, in 1945, Slim was faced by the Burma Area Army commanded by Lieutenant-General Kimura Heitaro. Kimura was a brilliant staff officer without any operational experience at a time when he was thrown against Slim in the defence of the 'Irrawaddy Shore'. He had spent his career not on the front line, like Mutaguchi, but on the staff and in highly political posts at the heart of the War Ministry. In 1935 as a major-general he became Section Chief at the Economics and Mobilization Bureau of the War Ministry, followed by a period as Chief of the Military Administration Bureau, also in the War Ministry. In April 1941 he was promoted to lieutenant-general and appointed Vice Minister of War, Prime Minister Tojo's right-hand man, a post he held until March 1943. It was this role more than any other that led to his trial and execution in 1948, on the charge of waging aggressive war. In 1943 he became a Member of the Planning Board and Total War Institute, before embarking for South-east Asia, undertaking several months in HQ Southern Army, Saigon before moving to Burma. A more conventional soldier than Mutaguchi, and entirely without combat experience, Kimura was completely unprepared for the violence and speed of Fourteenth Army's assault on his defences along the Irrawaddy, nor indeed of the subtlety of Slim's plan, which took him entirely by surprise. His forces were substantial, nevertheless, and his subordinate commanders were very experienced. He had the rebuilt Fifteenth Army in the centre around Mandalay, commanded by Lieutenant-General Katamura, who was blooded against the British Indian Army in Arakan in 1944. In the south, based on Meiktila, the experienced Twenty-eighth Army was commanded by Lieutenant-General Sakurai, who had commanded one of the two Japanese divisions in the invasion of Burma in 1942, and who had subsequently led Twenty-eighth Army throughout the Arakan fighting. In the north Lieutenant-General Honda, who had considerable experience fighting the Chinese, commanded Thirty-third Army, facing off the threat

An official photo taken in 1944. Slim hated self-publicity, as it went against every grain of his being, believing, perhaps naively, that victory in battle spoke louder than words. The greatest contrast with this approach can be observed in the attitude of the renowned self-publicist, Montgomery of Alamein who believed that if you didn't blow your own trumpet no one else would. (IWM, IND 3595)

from the American-led and supplied Chinese. He had a further two divisions in reserve – the 2nd and 49th Divisions – as well as seven battalions of the Burma National Army and Indian National Army, who proved to be considerably less reliable in action now that the Japanese were no longer in the ascendant.

But Kimura could do nothing against the relentless pressure placed on every point of his defences by Fourteenth Army, losing Meiktila by 3 March 1945 and having his counterattacks repeatedly repelled. Forced to order a general withdrawal on 28 March to prevent his forces in the central region being cut off, he attempted to give himself some breathing space by organizing defensive lines to be established at Pyawbwe and at Toungoo, on the edge of the Shan States. Unfortunately for him Slim's armour took little time to smash the Pyawbwe positions and at Toungoo the British had been long preparing guerrilla forces of Karens under the control of Force 136, who harried the Japanese lines of communication mercilessly. The Shan State operations by British special forces were a spectacular success for the advancing Allies and entirely undid Kimura's attempts to maintain the cohesion of his shattered army. Indeed, in April, with the consecutive collapse of both the Pyawbwe and Toungoo lines he lost control of both Fifteenth and Thirty-third Armies, as they disintegrated, the survivors streaming east and south-east towards southern Burma and Thailand and the final battles of the Sittang Bend.

Kimura, faced with the stark choice of defending Rangoon – which Southern Army in Saigon instructed him to do – or attempting to save what he could of his army in order to prepare for the defence of Thailand, explicitly ignored his instructions and ordered what remained of his forces to abandon Rangoon and to move towards Moulmein in preparation for defending south-east Burma. He abandoned Rangoon to the British on 26 April 1945, finally ordering his army to surrender between 20 and 23 August 1945.

# INSIDE THE MIND

As a man and as a leader Slim was approachable and accessible. He had a natural easiness about him. The journalist Frank Owen described him in 1945 as '53, burly, grey and going a bit bald. His mug is large and weather beaten, with a broad nose, jutting jaw, and twinkling hazel eyes. He looks like a well-to-do West Country farmer, and could be one.' George MacDonald Fraser's description of him as akin to a favourite uncle, was apt. He was not stuffy, and had a knack of creating an easy rapport with his men. He was one of those few men of real stature who never talk about themselves, it being unnecessary to advertise their own qualities. He was, at heart, a modest man. He listened before he spoke, rarely swore and never lost his temper in public. Major-General Ouvry Roberts, one of Scoones' divisional commanders at Imphal, who had observed Slim closely not just in Burma but also in Iraq,

At RAF Northolt with Omar Bradley in 1949. When he was CIGS Slim's relationship with Bradley (the US Army Chief of Staff in 1948 and from August 1949 the first Chairman of the (US) Joint Chiefs of Staff) was hugely important given the fragile state of global politics. On issues such as the Atomic bomb, the Korean War and the emergence of NATO Slim and Bradley, whose personalities were very similar, created a purposeful and productive modus vivendi between the British and US Armies. (Getty, 3353060)

Syria and Iran during 1941, considered that he was not just 'the finest British General of World War II... [but] also the most humble'. He was also intelligent, well-read and articulate. As with all other officers at the time who did not have the benefit of what was described euphemistically as 'private means' he struggled to live off his army salary, and so turned his hand to writing articles during the inter-war years for *Blackwood's Magazine* under the pseudonym of Anthony Mills.

He was a sociable man, but not enthusiastic about parties. He preferred the company of close friends to the enforced and artificial jollity of the crowd. He drank little, nursing a whisky and soda long after less disciplined souls had been obliged to retire from the fray, nor was he a religious man, regarding his Roman Catholicism to be an occasional obligation rather than a serious commitment.

Publicly reticent, he actively sought to remain out of the limelight. He positively detested publicity, providing a contrasting style to a commander like Montgomery. At a time when his own men were beginning to recognize in the architect of the Japanese defeat at Imphal/Kohima in 1944 a previously unheralded genius, he refused to accept even the most veiled accolade. 'He does not consider himself to be a Napoleon,' wrote Frank Owen, commenting on the standing in which he was held by his men. He reported that Slim observed that: 'A general's job is simply to make fewer mistakes than the other fellow. I try hard not to make too many mistakes.' Nevertheless, he recognized the importance of being seen by his men, and so he made a point of speaking to every combatant unit, or at least to its officers and NCOs, whenever he had the opportunity to get away from his headquarters. 'My platform was usually the bonnet of my jeep with the men collected anyhow around it,' he wrote. 'I often did three or four of these stump speeches in a day.' The result was a widespread confidence across Fourteenth Army that the show was in good hands. It is noteworthy that by 1945 Slim's army was 75 per cent Indian, Gurkha and East and West African, and only 25 per cent British. Unusually among many in his British peer group, but in common with his Indian Army colleagues, Slim was colour-blind. His 'non-ethnocentricity' was marked, and enabled him to deal impartially with his Chinese and American allies, as well as with the troops of many nations under his command. Even the acerbic, limey-hating 'Vinegar Joe' Stilwell was happy enough to report directly to Slim, even though this arrangement made a mockery of the proper channels of command. Professor Norman Dixon's study of military leadership, *On the Psychology of Military Incompetence*, concluded that the affection shown to Slim by British, Indian, Nepalese, African, Chinese and American troops led to his being loved by his polyglot army 'perhaps more than any other commander has been loved by his men since Nelson'.

Slim was honest, and admitted his mistakes. In *Defeat into Victory* he acknowledged two in particular. At Imphal he recalled his forward troops rather late, so that they had to fight their way back to the defensive ring around the north-eastern edge of the Imphal Plain. Then, at Kohima, he miscalculated both the speed and strength of the Japanese attack and very nearly lost the battle, were it not for the remarkable defence of the Kohima Ridge by a mixture of Territorial soldiers from the 4th Battalion, Royal West Kents, and a polyglot group of troops who had not expected to have to fight. Few other generals of the time would ever have admitted what Slim did both at the time and in the pages of his memoirs, that: 'I was, like other generals before me, saved from the consequences of my mistakes by the resourcefulness of my subordinate commanders and the stubborn valour of my troops.'

At Staff College, Camberley, with Montgomery, 1948. The relationship between these two men was never comfortable, as perhaps can be seen in this photograph, although they never worked together. They had diametrically different personalities. Montgomery scoffed that Slim was merely a 'sepoy general', insinuating that he was in a lesser league than him on the generalship front. Few of the members of Fourteenth Army would have agreed with Montgomery's verdict: the idea of 'Uncle Bernard' is inconceivable. (Getty, 2634717)

# WHEN THE WAR IS DONE

At the end of 1945 Slim returned to the UK when he became the Commandant of the Imperial Defence College for its first course since 1939. In 1948 he retired from the army. He had been approached by both India and Pakistan to become Commander-in-Chief of their respective armies after independence but refused and instead became Deputy Chairman of British Railways. However, in November 1948 the British Prime Minister Clement Attlee rejected the proposal by Viscount Montgomery that he should be succeeded as Chief of the Imperial General Staff by Lieutenant-General Sir John Crocker, and instead brought back Slim from retirement in the rank of field marshal in January 1949. John Slim, his son, was at the time attending a course at the School of Infantry in Warminster. He recalled that when the news was announced that 'Uncle Bill' was being brought back as CIGS the entire mess erupted into spontaneous applause.

He relinquished this position on 1 November 1952 after steering the army through the Korean War and the vast reduction of force structures attendant on the drawdown following the end of World War II. A few months later he began, with Aileen, the long journey to the Antipodes to take up his appointment as Governor General of Australia. Slim was a hugely popular choice for Governor General since he was an authentic war hero who had fought alongside Australians at Gallipoli and in the Middle East. In 1954 he was able to welcome Queen Elizabeth II on the first visit by a reigning monarch to Australia. It was while he was in Australia that *Defeat into Victory* made it into press.

As CIGS, 9 January 1950, leaving 10 Downing Street. Prime Minister Clement Attlee recalled Slim from his retirement job with British Rail in order to succeed Montgomery as CIGS. Montgomery had no wish to be succeeded by a flame brighter than his own, and worked strenuously to prevent the appointment. He failed. In his determination to appoint Slim, Attlee was firmly supported by the former Viceroy of India, Lord Mountbatten. Slim took up the appointment on 1 November 1948. (Getty, 3322002)

In 1959 Slim retired and he and Aileen returned to Britain, where on 15 July 1960 he was created 'Viscount Slim of Yarralumla in the Capital Territory of Australia and of Bishopston in the City and County of Bristol'. He was appointed Constable and Governor of Windsor Castle on 18 June 1964, a post hitherto reserved exclusively for members of the royal family. He died in London on 14 December 1970 and was given a full military funeral at St George's Chapel, Windsor. A remembrance plaque was placed in St Paul's Cathedral to Uncle Bill, but only in 1990 was a permanent memorial to him unveiled on Whitehall, outside the Ministry of Defence. There, for the first time, he receives enduring public recognition for his remarkable military achievements, his statue standing alongside those of Montgomery and Lord Alanbrooke: the three greatest British commanders of the war.

# A LIFE IN WORDS

Only a fraction of what has been written about other generals, some of whom were less capable commanders but more astute self-publicists, has been published about Slim. Indeed, this is only the fifth book exclusively to consider the command and leadership attributes of the man who led the largest ever British Army during World War II and who was responsible for two of Japan's greatest ever military defeats on land. The first to do so was Geoffrey Evans' *Slim as Military Commander* (Batsford: London, 1969), followed by Michael Calvert's thin volume entitled, merely, *Slim* (Ballantine: London, 1973). This was then followed by Ronald Lewin's superb biography, *Slim, The Standard Bearer* (Leo Cooper: London, 1976), which won the W. H. Smith Literary Award that same year. Fourth, the current author published *Slim, Master of War* (Constable: London, 2004), which evaluated Slim's generalship in Burma between 1942 and 1945 and argued that it formed the basis for a modern, innovative approach to warfighting. This argument was developed in *The Generals* (Constable: London, 2008). An important new analysis of Allied higher command in the war in the Far East can be found in Frank McLynn's *The Burma Campaign* (Bodley Head, 2010).

Essays on Slim as a commander (see bibliography) have been written by Geoffrey Evans, Brian Bond and Duncan Anderson, and a wide range of books include vignettes on Slim, some taken from personal experience of him at war. One of the most famous of these is George Macdonald Fraser's *Quartered Safe Out Here* (Harper Collins: London, 1992).

Slim wrote a best-selling account of his experience of war in Burma and India, published in London in 1956 by Cassell under the title *Defeat into Victory*. It was an instant publishing sensation in the United Kingdom with the first edition of 20,000 selling out almost immediately. It is widely regarded as a classic memoir of high command. Major-General D. R. Bateman wrote in *The Field*: 'Of all the world's greatest records of war and military adventure, this story must surely take its place among the greatest. It is told with a wealth of human understanding, a gift of vivid description, and a revelation of the indomitable spirit of the fighting man that can seldom have been equalled – let alone surpassed – in military history.' George Thompson in the *London Evening Standard* was as effusive in his praise: 'He has written the best general's book of World War II. Nobody who reads his account of the war, meticulously honest yet deeply moving, will doubt that here is a soldier of stature and a man among men.'

With Her Majesty the Queen in Canberra, 1954. Slim was a tremendously popular Governor General of Australia between 1952 and 1959. On 15 July 1960, he was created 'Viscount Slim of Yarralumla in the Capital Territory of Australia and of Bishopston in the City and County of Bristol'. (Getty, 3326291)

When it was published in the United States in 1961 it received similar reviews. *The Journal of Modern History* in 1963 considered it a work of 'wisdom, modesty, grace, and deep understanding', and 'an outstanding example of the best of British military memoirs'. The author John Masters, who served in Fourteenth Army, wrote in the *New York Times* on 19 November 1961 that it was 'a dramatic story with one principal character and several hundred subordinate characters,' arguing that Slim was 'an expert soldier and an expert writer'. The book remains a best seller today.

The following year Slim also published an anthology of speeches and lectures, loosely based on the theme of leadership, entitled *Courage and Other Broadcasts*. Then in 1959 Slim published his second book, *Unofficial History*, which bears out in full Masters' description of Slim as a superb writer. It was a deeply personal, honest though light-hearted account of events during his service in locations and at times missed by the history books. It received widespread acclaim. The author John Connell described it as 'for the most part uproarious fun. If Bill Slim hadn't been a first-rate soldier, what a short story writer he might have made.' For its part *The National Review* wrote: 'One of the most significant aspects of Field Marshal Slim's book is the affectionate respect he shows when he writes about British and Indian soldiers. He finds plenty to amuse him too. I doubt whether a kindlier or truer description of the contemporary soldier has been given anywhere than in *Unofficial History*... It is one of the most delightful and amusing books about modern campaigning I have ever read.'

At Churchill's funeral, 10 January 1965. At this stage Slim was the Governor and Constable of Windsor Castle. He was also 'flat out' (a favourite phrase of his) with a wide range of activities, including chairmanship of several companies, his close involvement in the creation of St George's House and his duties as a Knight of the Garter. He worked well with Churchill. In 1952 Churchill remarked to Lord Moran: 'When a man cannot distinguish a great from a small event he is no use. Now Slim is quite different. I can work with him.' (Corbis, HU045589)

The literature of the Burma Campaign (which, of course, includes the battles for Arakan, Imphal and Kohima) is vast (and growing). For dedicated students of the campaign the first step must be a visit to the Burma Campaign Memorial Library, the most comprehensive collection of sources on the war in Burma and India probably anywhere in the world and the brainchild of Major Gordon Graham MC, which is housed in the library of the School of Oriental and African Studies, Thornhaugh Street, Russell Square, London WC1H OXG. Other excellent collections are held in the London Library (which is membership only, but well worth the investment), and the Prince Consort's Library, Aldershot.

# FURTHER READING

Anderson, Duncan, 'Slim' in John Keegan (ed.) *Churchill's Generals* Weidenfeld and Nicholson: London, 1991

——, 'The Very Model of a Modern Manoeuvrist General: William Slim and the Exercise of High Command in Burma' in Gary Sheffield and Geoffrey Till (eds.) *The Challenges of High Command* Palgrave: Basingstoke, 2003

Swinson, Arthur, *Kohima* Cassell: London, 1966

Allen, Louis, *Burma: The Longest War* Dent, London, 1984

——, 'The Campaigns in Asia and the Pacific' in J. Gooch (ed.) *Decisive Campaigns of the Second World War* Frank Cass: London, 1990

Barnett, Corelli, 'The Impact of Surprise and Initiative in War' *Royal United Services Institute Journal* London, June 1984

Bidwell, Shelford, *The Chindit War: The Campaign in Burma, 1944* Hodder and Stoughton: London, 1979

Bond, Brian (ed.), *British and Japanese Military Leadership in the Far Eastern War, 1941–1945* Cass: London, 2004

Brett-James, Antony, and Evans, Geoffrey, *Imphal* Macmillan: London, 1962

Callahan, Raymond, *Burma 1942–45* Davis-Poynter: London, 1978

Calvert, Michael, *Slim* Pan/Ballantine: London, 1973

Evans, Geoffrey, *Slim as Military Commander* Batsford: London, 1969

——, 'Slim' in Michael Carver (ed.), *The War Lords: Military Commanders of the Twentieth Century* Weidenfeld and Nicholson: London, 1976

Dixon, Norman *On the Psychology of Military Incompetence* Jonathan Cape: London, 1976

Forty, George, *XIV Army At War* Ian Allan: London, 1982

Fraser, George MacDonald, *Quartered Safe Out Here* Harper Collins: London, 1992

Hickey, Michael, *The Unforgettable Army: Slim's XIVth Army in Burma* Spellmount: Tunbridge Wells, 1992

Latimer, Jon, *Burma, The Forgotten War* John Murray: London, 2004

Lewin, Ronald, *Slim, The Standard Bearer* Leo Cooper: London, 1976

Lunt, James, *'A Hell of a Licking': The Retreat from Burma 1941–2* Collins: London, 1986

Lyall Grant, Ian, and Tamayama, Kazuo, *Burma 1942: The Japanese Invasion. Both sides tell the Story of a Savage Jungle War* The Zampi Press: Chichester, 1999

Lyman, Robert, *Slim, Master of War: Burma and the Birth of Modern Warfare* Constable: London, 2004

——, 'The Art of Manouevre at the Operational Level of war: Lieutenant General W. J. Slim and Fourteenth Army, 1944–45' in Gary Sheffield and Geoffrey Till (eds.) *The Challenges of High Command* Palgrave: Basingstoke, 2003

——, *First Victory: Britain's Forgotten Struggle in the Middle East, 1941* Constable: London, 2006

——, *The Generals* Constable: London, 2008

Masters, John, *The Road Past Mandalay* Michael Joseph: London, 1961

McKie, Ronald, *Echoes From Forgotten Wars* Collins: Sydney, 1980

McLynn, Frank, *The Burma Campaign* The Bodley Head: London, 2010

Owen, Frank, *The Campaign in Burma* HMSO: London, 1946

Perrett, Bryan, *Seize and hold: Master strokes on the battlefield* Arms and Armour Press: London, 1994

Sixsmith, E. K. G., *British Generalship in the Twentieth Century* Arms and Armour Press: London, 1970

Slim, William, *Defeat into Victory* Cassell: London, 1956

——, *Unofficial History* Cassell: London, 1959

——, *Courage and other broadcasts* Cassell: London, 1957

——, 'Higher Command in War' *US Army Military Review*, May 1990

——, 'Campaign of the Fourteenth Army 1944–1945' *Australian Army Journal*, August 1950

——, 'Liberty and Discipline' *US Army Journal*, October 1976

Smurthwaite, David (ed.), *The Forgotten War* National Army Museum: London, 1992

Smith, E. D., *Battle for Burma* Batsford: London, 1979

Thompson, Julian, *The Imperial War Museum Book of the War in Burma 1942–1945* Pan: London, 2002

——, *The Lifeblood of War: Logistics in Armed Conflict* Brasseys: London, 1991

Woodburn Kirby, Stanley, *The War Against Japan,* Volume II, HMSO: London, 1958

——, *The War Against Japan,* Volume III, HMSO: London, 1962

Ziegler, Philip, *Mountbatten* Collins: London, 1985

# INDEX